Paul Ferrini reconnec to that place where even our deepest wounds can be healed.

JOAN BORYSENKO

Paul Ferrini's wonderful books show us a way to walk lightly with joy on planet Earth.

GERALD JAMPOLSKY

Paul Ferrini's work is a must read for all people who are ready to take responsibility for their own healing.

JOHN BRADSHAW

Paul Ferrini's books are the most important I have read. I study them like a Bible.

ELISABETH KÜBLER-ROSS

Paul Ferrini's writing will inspire you to greater insights and understandings, to more clarity and a grander resolve to make changes in your life that can truly change the world.

NEALE DONALD WALSCH

Paul Ferrini is an important teacher in the new millenium. Reading his work has been a major awakening for me.

IYANLA VANZANT

Paul Ferrini is a modern day Kahlil Gibran— poet, mystic, visonary, teller of truth.

LARRY DOSSEY

I feel that this work comes from a continuous friendship with the deepest Part of the Self. I trust its wisdom.

COLEMAN BARKS

Book Design by Lisa Carta

Library of Congress Card Number 2011905242
ISBN # 978-1-879159-85-3

Manufactured in the United States of America

HEALING YOUR LIFE

A 12 Step Guide

*to Bringing Love, Power & Purpose
into Your Life*

TABLE OF CONTENTS

PREFACE

Eight years ago, I invited my readers to join me in Florida for a series of intensive retreats. People came from all over the world to learn and practice the principles of unconditional love, self-healing and forgiveness.

Many participants attended three retreats in just three months and the intensity of their participation yielded powerful results. Emotional wounds began to heal. People began to drop their patterns of self-betrayal and step into their power and purpose.

We were all amazed at our experience and wanted to share it with others. So, at the urging of my students, I began to put together an intensive, experiential workshop that captured and integrated the most important elements of over 35 years of my teaching and writing experience. *The Real Happiness Workshop* did what we asked it to do. It facilitated deep emotional healing and spiritual transformation for others.

During the last four years many teachers have been trained and our *Real Happiness Workshop Intensives* have been offered with great success in many countries. The curriculum has been translated into a number of languages and the work continues to expand. The teachers have truly become instruments for the extension of this important work to others. By showing up and holding the space of unconditional love and acceptance, they have created communities where people feel safe to heal and to transform their lives.

This is the first time that this curriculum has been offered to people in a trade book form. It is my hope that by offering it in this manner, more people will have access to the teaching and will want to come and do the work in person with one of our certified teachers.

In our experience, most people do not easily heal their family of origin wounds and break through their patterns of self-betrayal. Most people need a consistent support structure that keeps them energetically focused on their healing process. That is why we have spent the last eight years developing an international healing community that actively supports people in the work of emotional healing and empowerment.

This community is available to you as a resource. The support of other like-minded and emotionally courageous individuals will move you forward more deeply and with more profound results.

You do not have to live in sacrifice, without love and support in your life. This work and the community that stands behind it can help you open up to a life of genuine healing and empowerment. You can learn to love yourself from the inside out, thereby initiating a process of giving and receiving that will transform your life. You can end your suffering and connect with your joy. You can find your passion in life and learn to nurture and express your gifts. You can learn to be the bringer of love to your own experience and attract more and more love into your life. You can fulfill your life purpose and live with your partner in an equal, mutually empowered relationship.

All the gifts of life and love are possible for you. You need only do your part and open your heart to receive them. This book will help you begin. As you undertake this journey, know that we are with you, holding the space for your healing and empowerment.

Love and blessings,

Paul Ferrini

Roadmap of Twelve Steps to Healing & Transformation

* The *Real Happiness Roadmap* is divided into 3 Phases, 6 stages, and 12 steps. Stages are shown above, even though they are not referenced in this book.

INTRODUCTION

The Roadmap to Healing & Transformation

Our Pain is a Wake Up Call

When we were first developing our *Roadmap of Twelve Steps to Healing and Transformation* I asked my students "Where do you think the roadmap begins?" Many people said that connecting to love was the first step. That made sense. But I wanted them to go deeper. Please answer the question personally. "Where did healing begin for you? What drew you to come to these retreats?"

Celia immediately answered, "For me it all began with feeling my pain." When she said that we all felt a deep resonance. For most of us the journey to healing began when our pain rose up and refused to be repressed, pushed away or ignored anymore. For most of us, pain was the wake-up call. It showed us what was off-track in our lives, what needed to be addressed for healing to come.

In our world, pain is not looked at as a messenger. We want to make it go away. We use all kinds of substances to override our pain or anesthetize it. Alcohol, prescription and recreational drugs, even food, work or sex become a way to avoid our pain or deny it. In our attempt to find pleasure and escape pain, it does not occur to us that we need to listen to the message our pain brings to us.

But Celia was right. We do need to listen. Until we know what hurts and why it hurts, we will have little motivation to take the transformational journey.

Meeting our Shadow

So in Phase One of our work, we stop denying or dulling down our pain and begin to feel it and hear the message that it conveys. This brings up a lot of shame for everyone. We all have developed social and spiritual masks that we hide behind, pretending to be happy when we feel like crap inside. Acknowledging our pain to ourselves and others means taking off our mask and telling the truth about how we feel. It means being emotionally honest and vulnerable.

Of course, we are afraid to be in the world without our mask. In the world, we are often crucified, judged and blamed for any weakness we have. It isn't safe to let people see who we really are and how we really feel. We are afraid and ashamed of what is inside. Like Adam and Eve, we hide our fear and shame and pretend to be happy when we are not.

In our work, we carefully create a space of unconditional love and acceptance so that it feels safe to share our pain. We use the *Affinity Process Guidelines** so that each one of us owns our experience and does not project our fear and our shame onto others. We learn to speak and listen from the heart. We learn to trust each other with the truth of our experience,

---

*See my books *Living in the Heart* and *The Keys to the Kingdom* for more information on *The Affinity Group Process*.

so that we don't have to hide anymore. We come out of the closet. We allow ourselves to be heard and seen. We allow ourselves to be loved and accepted just the way we are.

The major work of Phase One is the creation of a healing community, a safe space, in which we can meet our shadow and that of others in a compassionate way. As we tell the truth, we see that our experience is not that different from that of others. Our pain is their pain. Our trials and tribulations, our judgments of ourselves, our feelings of unworthiness are not very different from theirs. We share a similar psychological world in which our fear and shame rise up repeatedly.

For years we thought we were the only one who felt so inadequate. We thought everyone else out there was happy and well-adjusted. We did not know that we were just seeing the masks that they were wearing. But now, in the loving, non-judgmental space of our healing community, where it is safe to take off our masks, we understand that we are not the only ones in pain. We are not the only ones dealing with fear and shame. We are not the only ones who feel guilty, afraid, and unworthy of love. Every person in the room feels the same way. This is just the first time we have shared our pain with others. This is a milestone for all of us, and it creates the momentum we need for coming out of denial.

We go from being in a world in which we cannot admit our fears and our weaknesses to being in a world where it is safe to be honest with others. We go from being in a world in which we must hide the truth to being in a world where the truth can be acknowledged by everyone.

In Phase One of the work, we come face to face with our pain. We share it with others. We witness the universality of our pain, and learn to be gentle with ourselves and others. Instead of being ashamed of our feelings, we learn to accept them and move through them. We support each other in holding a compassionate space where our fears can be faced. We learn to look at our shadow material through the eyes of love. That means that we no longer need to be threatened by the unhealed aspects of ourselves or others. We no longer need to deny our pain and project it onto others.

Together, we can make a space for healing. Together we can create a loving environment and a culture of forgiveness that enables us to see and own our judgments so that we can stop attacking others.

Connecting with love becomes an important aspect of our Phase One work. We cannot look at our shadow and that of others if we are not feeling loved and accepted. Without the connection to love, we either reject/deny the shadow (as we have done before) or we identify with it and think it is who we are. We either turn away from our healing journey because it is too scary, or we enter the underworld without carrying the torch that illuminates it. Neither choice is constructive.

We need to take the time we need to gather the light and love of compassionate awareness before we enter the underworld to come face to face with our shadow.

Phase Two of the *Roadmap to Healing and Transformation* will bring us face to face with our deepest wounds and dysfunctional beliefs about ourselves. We need to be ready to look at all this. We need to know that we can hold our fear and our shame in a gentle, loving way. We need to know that we can witness and accept all these rejected and denied aspects of ourselves. That is what helps us reclaim and integrate them. That is how wholeness is restored to our psyche.

The Journey into the Underworld

Have no illusions. It takes courage to make the journey within. In Phase Two we are asked to look at our mommy and daddy wounds and to walk through the fear and the shame attached to them. We are asked to see where our patterns of self-betrayal begin in childhood and how they continue into adulthood, influencing the choices we make in our work and relationships. We are asked to see the whole setup of our lives: how we gave our power away and allowed others to make decisions for us, or how we showed up as a caretaker or control freak, taking away the power of others and inappropriately deciding for them,

We are asked to see the whole generational cycle of abuse, how victims become victimizers, how we become Mommy or Daddy and pass the wound we received from them onto our own children. It isn't pleasant or pretty stuff to look at. That's why most people don't take the journey, or, if they do, they turn back before they see the light at the end of the tunnel.

It takes great courage to feel and transform your core wound. You could not do this as a child. It was too scary and overwhelming. You did not have the ego strength or self-confidence to face it. You did not have the support of others. It was a lonely time and you did what all of us do: you shoved it, denied it, hid it, buried it out of sight and out of mind. That's okay. What else could you do?

But even though you made it go away for a while, it inevitably comes back. Your wound and patterns of self-betrayal come up in every close relationship you have.

Your children, your parents, your siblings, your coworkers, even strangers you meet on the street push your buttons. You are triggered when you least expect it. In spite of your attempt to hide your feelings behind your mask, anger (even rage) may bleed through. You may abandon the people you love. Or you may allow yourself to be emotionally or physically abused. All this happens in your life or in the life of someone close to you. It is commonplace. Yet no one wants to talk about.

There is a conspiracy of silence. No one wants to go there. And then people wonder why someone goes out, buys a machine gun and shoots ten people at work or at school, or murders their spouse or children. This is grisly stuff. If it is not dealt with, if it is not faced and healed, the cycle of violence proliferates.

Violence begins in our hearts and minds. It extends outward into our families and communities. It plays out in wars and genocidal actions. It permeates the collective consciousness. People want to kill and exterminate what they don't understand and accept. They want to destroy the shadow in others. They demonize each other so that they don't have to feel the pain of their trespass. They think they are killing gooks or devils, not human beings. But in truth, they are killing their mothers and fathers. They are killing their children. They are killing their brothers and sisters. All because they hate themselves. All because they have not been able to look at their own shadow with compassion. All because they never learned to bring love to the wounded child within.

Healing the Wounded Child

In Phase Two we learn to reclaim the rejected aspects of ourselves. We see what we don't like, what we are ashamed of. We use the mirror that other people hold up to us to see what we condemn within ourselves. We learn to see and show up for that hurt child within, the one who feels rejected and unworthy of love, the one who feels that she doesn't even have the right to breathe the air. The one who believes that she is bad, evil, dirty, ugly, unlovable. We learn to sit with the child while she screams or rages out. We learn to follow her patiently when she runs away and hides. We learn to raise her up off the ground when she tries to grovel at our feet.

No matter how hard it is, no matter how long it takes, we learn to show up for that little kid and get our arms around him or her. We learn to say "I am not going to reject you or abandon you anymore. I am not going to make you wrong, criticize you or find fault with you. I am not going to do all those things that Mommy or Daddy did to you and that I learned to do to you from their example. I am not going to be the one who attacks you. I am going to stay here with you and learn to be your friend. I am going to accept you, hold the space for you, learn to love you, so that you can heal your pain, so that you can grow up and express your gifts. I am going to be the compassionate Mommy and Daddy that you never had."

Needless to say, this is a profound healing process, and it does not happen quickly.

It takes a lot of patience and conviction to show up for yourself in this way. But nothing else will work. You are the bringer of love to your own experience. No one else can do that for you. Not Mommy or Daddy. Not husband or wife. You are the one who has to learn to bring love. Only your love will heal your wound.

Many people try to find shortcuts to healing, but these shortcuts are always some form of denial. They try to make the pain go away. They don't invite it in so that its transformational message can be heard.

Shortcuts shame and punish the child all over again. They tell him, "You aren't spiritual or you would already be healed. You need to do this or do that, say this or say that." It's all a bunch of mumbo jumbo, but the child believes it all because he thinks he is damaged goods and needs to be fixed. He is only too happy to swallow another plan for his redemption.

Of course, none of these plans will work. They are doomed to fail, and when they do they merely reinforce the child's pain and the belief that he can't do anything right.

The only thing that works is love and acceptance. Through love and acceptance we build a relationship of trust with the child. And, gradually over time, he is re-parented and grows up healed and empowered. This is a process that takes years, not days or weeks or months.

That fact should not be a dissuading factor to you. If you want real healing and real happiness, it is going to take time, patience and commitment. If you realize that, you will come prepared, and you will be successful.

Real Healing and Transformation

Success on the healing journey means real transformation, not just a cosmetic fix. Real healing happens from the inside out, and it extends to every area of your life. Phase Three of the Roadmap is all about empowerment and results.

Your relationship to yourself is transformed because you have learned to bring love to the child within. You have learned to stay connected to him or her, to be emotionally honest and congruent. When fear rises, you know how to hold it compassionately. When judgments come, you hold them gently and bring love to the one who feels insecure or unworthy.

Because you have developed a loving relationship with yourself, real happiness is possible in work and in relationships. You are able to recognize, nurture and express your creative gifts. You can connect with your heart's desire and do what you love to do, bringing inspiration and joy to others. You are able to attract and maintain a loving, equal relationship with a partner who shares your life and joins you in your healing journey.

You learn to hear and trust your guidance, to take appropriate risks and walk through the open doors in your life. You can feel your life unfolding from the inside out. The people you need to meet are drawn to you. The resources and support that you need fall into place without a lot of deliberation or effort. You are flexible and move with the flow of the universe. What used to be hard now becomes easy. What used to be a struggle becomes effortless. You no longer live in lack and sacrifice, but in joy and abundance.

Your love for yourself is so strong and steady that everyone around you can feel it. People are drawn to you for guidance, comfort and support. People who have wounds similar to yours arrive at the door to your home, your office, your church or temple. Naturally and spontaneously, you begin to give back to others all the gifts that you have received on your own healing journey.

Whether formally or informally, you begin to serve the greater good and the larger plan for healing on the planet. You do your part, whatever it is. You step into your life purpose and play the unique role that you are able to play. Your gifts and talents, your wisdom and strength are placed in service. Through you, others heal and discover the truth within themselves.

Having become the bringer of love to your own experience, the universe supports you in stepping forward as a spiritual guide for others. You hold the torch of unconditional love with confidence, pointing the way and lighting the path for others. Your will and the great will of the universal creator become one and the same.

As healing comes to your heart, heaven comes to earth, and peace comes to the world in which you live. May your experience with this Roadmap be as powerful and as transforming as it has been for all of us who have taken the journey.

Namaste.

PART ONE

Awakening

Real Happiness Roadmap

PHASE ONE

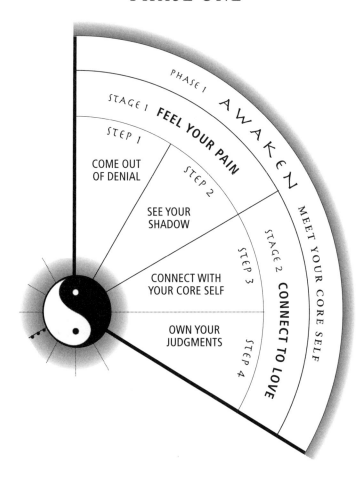

PHASE 1   AWAKEN

STAGE 1   **FEEL YOUR PAIN**

STEP 1   COME OUT OF DENIAL

STEP 2   SEE YOUR SHADOW

STAGE 2   MEET YOUR CORE SELF

STEP 3   CONNECT WITH YOUR CORE SELF

STAGE 2   **CONNECT TO LOVE**

STEP 4   OWN YOUR JUDGMENTS

Come Out of Denial

GOAL

Feel your pain and see it as a wake-up call.

STRATEGY

*Drop your mask. Open your heart. Get in touch
with your feelings and share them with others.*

The difficult but important truth is that you can't heal until you acknowledge your pain, your fear, and your shame. You can't heal until you stop hiding your negative feelings and stop pretending to be happy when you are not. You have to be authentic to be happy. You have to take off your mask and be real. You have to come out of the closet.

Pain is a wake-up call. Therefore, feeling and acknowledging your pain is the first step in the healing process. Anything that prevents you from feeling your pain and discovering its source is an act of denial. It is an attempt to ignore the call of your heart and soul to awaken and heal.

All addictions/compulsions are a form of denial. They anesthetize your pain or help you escape from it. As long as you are an addict, you won't feel the depth of your pain, and you will have little incentive to heal it.

Taking off Your Mask

Your mask or persona helps you gain social approval. It helps you to appear to be normal and well-adjusted, even if you aren't. It hides your pain and shows people an edited version of you. They don't see your fear, your shame, your grief, your self-judgment. They don't see how your heart hurts or how your mind is gripped by anxiety. In other words, your mask hides your shadow material. It is like make-up or hair spray. It hides your zits and makes your unruly hair sit down even on a bad hair day. It makes everything look better than it is so that the shadow can stay hidden.

The cosmetic industry benefits greatly from our attempt to deny the shadow. People have face lifts, belly tucks and breast implants because they don't feel comfortable with the sags and wrinkles of an aging body. They want a perfect body and a perfect life. Of course, the attempt to find perfection in the body or the world is bound to fail. The body withers and dies. The world is an unsteady place. There is no security here.

Real happiness cannot be found on the outside. It can only be found within. It can only be found by developing a loving relationship with yourself. And you can develop such a relationship only if you accept yourself, warts and all.

That means that you need to make peace with your shadow. You have to learn to see and to love all those aspects of you — physical, emotional and mental — that are un-ideal and challenging for yourself or others. You have to be willing to see not only where the body sags or extends outward inelegantly, but where your heart hurts or feels sad. You have to learn to get your arms around your whole experience, both high and low, good and bad, light and shadow.

Mask and Shadow

People may love your mask, but they don't necessarily see, accept or know what is underneath the mask. You yourself may not know the deeper, more primitive part of you. You may be disconnected from your emotional body and the pains and yearnings of your heart.

Your shadow is locked away behind your mask. Usually it is unconscious, which is why very few people are in touch with it. Generally, you see it only when you are triggered and your pain erupts. This is often sudden and surprising. You witness unhealed wounds you did not know that you had.

Our relationships inevitably push our buttons, and our pain inevitably leaks through our masks. Like most of us, you are probably trying to avoid this eruption of your shadow because you do not want to deal with your pain or the pain of others.

Society rewards you for having a good mask and living behind it. It is all about "saving face." It is all about looking good, even if you don't feel good. It is all about denying the shadow and not looking at your pain and self-betrayal.

Taking your mask off is therefore a revolutionary act. It is the first step in the process of healing your pain and creating an integration between shadow and persona.

Coming Out of Your Shell

Some people never get a good mask. They don't conform to norms very easily. When people judge or criticize them, they run away. They withdraw into an emotional shell. They hide there and remain invisible so that no one can criticize them, reject them or try to fix them.

While the mask is about getting social acceptance by showing our "good" side, the shell is about isolating from others so that they do not shame us (make us "bad" or "wrong") or attack us. Some of us develop masks. Some of us build shells. Sometimes we do both at the same time or at different times in our lives.

The shell builder usually does not have much of a social life. Her needs for belonging are not met. She would rather be independent and free than risk the loss of her freedom by conforming to the ideas and expectations of others.

When you wear a mask, others cannot see who you really are. You show them a False Self. When you hide in a shell, people can't be intimate with you. You hide from them because you are afraid of criticism or rejection. As you probably know, mask-making and shell-building start at a very early age.

This first step in your healing process is about coming out of whatever denial mechanism you have adopted. It asks you to take off your mask or to come out of your shell. It asks you to be visible to yourself and to others, just the way you are.

The Power of a Healing Community

Step One asks you to come out of the closet. It asks you stop hiding or pretending to be someone else and start being honest about who you are. You don't have to live a lie anymore. In fact, the reason you are in pain is precisely because you are living a lie. You are not being honest about who you are.

Being honest means acknowledging your pain to yourself and others. It means beginning to see all those parts of yourself that you have not yet learned to love. It means facing your fear and walking through your shame.

Of course, this takes courage on your part. And it requires an environment where it is safe to be yourself. It requires the creation of a loving community where you and others can heal your wounds and to step into your power and purpose.

A healing community offers a long-awaited antidote to the family of origin experience. Whether overtly or subtly, you were wounded in your family of origin. It wasn't your parents' fault. They were wounded too and were just teaching you what they were taught by their parents. This is not about finding fault with your parents or trying to make them responsible for your pain. That is a waste of time. It leads to victimhood, not to empowerment.

Yet you do not want to be in denial about your past. To the extent that you did not feel safe in your family or accepted by your parents and siblings, you learned to put on a mask or build a shell. That is where you began to betray yourself or isolate from others. That is where you learned to live a lie or disconnect from your feelings.

Now, as you come out of denial and are willing to feel your feelings, you need a loving family in which feelings are accepted and people are encouraged to be themselves. The healing community extends its loving arms around you as you come out of your shell or take off your mask. It encourages you to be honest and authentic. It invites you to share your inner truth with others.

Creating a Support Group

Hopefully you are reading this book with a group of like minded people who are ready to heal and be empowered. Ideally, the work presented in this book is done in a small group of eight to ten people who meet every week for at least twelve weeks. If you do not have such a group, I encourage you to complete our Facilitator Training and start a group in your community. At our trainings, you will experience this work in depth over three weekends. You will find it a life-changing experience. The training will anchor you deeply in the concepts and spiritual practices presented here. It will help you awaken, heal and come into your power and purpose. Then, you will be ready to share this work with others.

Four Ways of Staying in Denial

There are four primary ways in which you deny your pain:

1. You wear your mask

2. You crawl into your shell

3. You become addicted to substances that mask your pain.

4. You intellectualize your feelings.

You may have one, two, three or even all four of these denial mechanisms. Which mechanisms of denial do you have? Understanding the ways in which you live in denial is essential for beginning to wake up and take responsibility for your life.

All attempts to escape your pain by medicating it, denying it, or avoiding it are bound to fail. When you run away from your pain, you create more pain. Only when you face your pain can you move through it.

Please don't be afraid of your pain anymore. See it as your ally. Your pain is a wake-up call. It tells you what needs to change, heal or shift in your life.

Two Tips for Feeling & Moving Through Your Pain

1. Stay out of your head. Stop analyzing, intellectualizing, or seeking to justify your feelings. That's just a way of pushing the pain away. Just tune into how it feels.

2. Drop your mask. Break through your shell of isolation. Share your pain with others when it is safe to do so. When you have the courage to share your pain, you realize that you are not the only one who is suffering. This helps you to move through some of your shame and creates a community that supports your healing.

Important Questions to Ask Yourself

➤ Do I have a mask, a shell, or both?

➤ What does my mask look like and when do I wear it?

➤ Is there a place where I feel safe enough to take my mask off?

➤ What does my shell look like and when do I retreat into it?

➤ Does my shell keep me isolated from others? Is this the price I have to pay to feel safe?

➤ Is it hard for me to drop my mask/come out my shell and share my pain with others?

➤ What addictions do I have that numb my pain or enable me to avoid it?

➤ Do I intellectualize my feelings so I don't have to feel my pain?

2

See Your Shadow

GOAL

*Accept and integrate darkness
and light in your psyche.*

STRATEGY

Look with compassion. Be gentle with yourself.
See without judging or beating yourself up.

The shadow is the dark side of self. The persona (or mask) is the bright side of self. Like most people, you try to show people your bright side and hide your dark side. Yet this is not completely honest or authentic. Part of you is discounted, ignored and kept hidden or unconscious.

To be authentic and real, you have to embrace all of who you are — dark and light, strengths and weaknesses, what you like and what you do not like. When shadow and persona integrate, wholeness comes to the psyche, and real happiness is possible.

The shadow is the seat of your pain. It is where your fear and your shame live.

You try to hide your shadow behind your mask, but it doesn't work. That's because you project your unconscious shadowy material outward onto others. They react to your unconscious wound-driven words and behavior and you react to theirs. So your shadow (and theirs) does not stay hidden, but is mirrored back to you by others. Others show you the primitive, unhealed aspects of yourself that you are not conscious of and need to learn to recognize, love and accept.

Projection and Triggers

Inevitably, you see in others what you do not want to see or acknowledge in yourself. If you are not willing to encounter the shadow by looking within, you will see it outside yourself. It will be reflected back to you by others.

You don't want to look at the shadow, but you have no choice. Anything that is unhealed about you will be externalized, and you will see it in the words and actions of other people who trigger you.

As a result, your pain consists not only of your fear and shame, learned in childhood, but also of your ongoing judgments of others (projected shame) and anger at others (projected fear). That is why every judgment you have and every expression of anger must be forgiven. You can't heal if you can't forgive.

When Jesus told us "judge not lest you be judged," he was telling us an important truth. For every time we find fault with another person, we are making ourselves guilty. Each one of us is judge, jury and executioner.

The *Spiritual Law of Equality* (see my book *The Laws of Love*) tells you that you cannot hurt another without hurting yourself. This is true not just figuratively, but literally. You always treat yourself as you treat others. If you offer love, love returns to you. But if you offer criticism or rejection, it will return to you as well. As you give, so do you receive. This is the law of life.

It is a mistake to think that you or anyone can prosper by lying, cheating, criticizing or taking unfair advantage of another. What comes around, goes around. The chickens return to their roost. That is just the way it is. If you don't know that yet, sooner or later you will find out.

But why wait to put spiritual principle to work in your life? Do unto others as you would have them do unto you. Give as you would like to receive. Serve as you would like to be served. Love as you would like to be loved, freely and without conditions.

Why it is so Hard to Love Others

Many of us have the best of intentions. We really try to love others. And we are often successful in loving the people who share our values and are nice to us. But as soon as someone comes into our energy field and challenges us, judges us, looks at us disapprovingly, we go ballistic. The rage that comes out when we are triggered shocks us. Where does this anger come from?

The answer is not difficult. It comes from fear and shame, the bedrock of our shadow. Bottom line: we are afraid that someone might hurt us (fear) or make us wrong/bad (shame). Fear and shame are rooted in our childhood wounds. We were all afraid of our parents and other authority figures. They were bigger and stronger than us. And they too were filled with fear. When they went into fear, we followed with a vengeance. When they judged us or criticized us, we internalized the message.

There are layers upon layers of fear and shame that we are all carrying around. When that fear and shame get triggered by a parental or authority figure, we lose it big time. All of the anger and self-hatred we have stored inside since childhood comes rising up. Or, if we have been taught to repress and deny our anger, we shut down emotionally or sink into depression.

So we learn soon enough that loving other people isn't easy. In fact, it sometimes seems like an impossible task. We may be able to love some people, but there are others whom we hate or judge. We feel compelled to attack, reject or abandon them. We aren't proud of this, but we don't know how to turn it around. We don't know how to love others unconditionally.

Loving and Accepting the Shadow

The truth is that we will never be able to love anyone else unconditionally unless and until we are able to love ourselves without conditions. That means that we need to learn to accept our own dark side and learn to hold it compassionately. We need to look at our fear, our shame, our anger, our judgments, our addictions and compulsions, our trespasses against others with understanding and acceptance. We need to look with compassion at our own wounds and the wounds of our parents. We need to see how the chain of abuse is passed on from generation to generation.

We do this not to wallow in our pain, but to understand its source. Once we can feel compassion for the hurt child within, once we can learn to take the child into our arms and give him the love and acceptance he so desperately wants, we begin to transform our lives from the inside out. The shadow self begins to integrate with the persona and the division in the psyche begins to heal.

As we make peace with our own shadow, we are not so easily triggered by the shadow side of others. We don't react to their judgment, criticism, shame or blame. We know this is coming from their own wounds. This is their pain, not ours. We don't have to take it on. But we can understand it and can hold the space for them, because we have learned to hold the space for ourselves.

Loving and accepting our own shadow is the doorway to loving others without conditions. It does not happen overnight. It requires great patience and courage. It takes us years of spiritual practice to learn to show up for ourselves in a loving way. But once we have begun to do that, it is not hard to show up for others.

The point is that we cannot put the cart before the horse. We cannot try to love others before we learn to love ourselves. Self love is the engine of transformation. And shadow work is the curriculum.

To project our fear and shame onto others takes us into the drama of the world. There all of our energy goes into survival and self-protection. There our fear and anxiety are intensified. Yet, no matter how many defenses we erect, we can never feel safe.

Real safety is found only when we make peace with our own shadow. Then we do not attract the shadow energy of others. We stay in our hearts. We learn to love others even when they do not love us. When others attempt to shame and blame us, we turn the other cheek. We invite them to see us as we truly are, as an equal brother or sister.

Learning from the Shadow

When you encounter the shadow of another person with its wound driven energy of shame and blame, you have an opportunity to do intense spiritual practice. Can you see their innocence behind the Shadow? Can you see and know your own innocence even though they would make you guilty?

When people shame you and blame you, do you see that they are just showing you their own self-hatred and guilt? Would they attack you if they loved themselves and knew that they were innocent? Probably not!

No one blames another unless he feels less than and unworthy (shame). No one attacks another unless he is afraid of being hurt physically, emotionally or mentally (fear). Do you see his attack as an attempt to hurt you or as a call for love? Is he telling you that he does not feel loved and that he needs your love?

The people who push your buttons are your best teachers. They mirror back to you the unhealed parts of yourself. If you can look behind the shadow to the light they have within, you can reinforce your own innocence even as you behold theirs. You can know that in every moment both you and your brother or sister are worthy of love.

If you think otherwise, then you have fear or shame coming up. In that case, it is time to do your spiritual work.

You cannot justify *not* accepting or loving others. There is no one here who does not deserve your love and acceptance. Some people may be difficult to love. They may challenge you. They may have qualities that reflect your own unconscious negative beliefs. But that just provides you with an opportunity to make your own shadow conscious. It enables you to bring love to a part of yourself you have never liked or accepted.

When someone who is difficult is in your energy field demanding your attention, you can be sure that s/he is there for you to learn something important. Find a way to see her with love, and you bring that love to the deepest and most wounded aspects of yourself.

As you make friends with the shadow, you no longer have to project it onto others. Then you can heal your relationships with the people who used to trigger you. Then, your whole life begins to transform.

Looking with Compassion

The key to the process of integrating your shadow is to see it with compassion. That means that you need to look at your judgments of yourself and others without beating yourself up. You need to see the dark, unhealed aspects of self, without making them bad or evil.

When you see with acceptance and compassion, you bring the light to the dark places in your psyche. This illuminates them and creates the potential for their integration.

On the other hand, when you see with judgment, you push the shadow back into the darkness. You make it bad, evil, unacceptable, and yes, you hide it from sight once again.

The reason that many people do not heal is that they deny their pain and shame and push the shadow down underneath their mask, showing people their bright side and hiding their dark side. As a result, they never acknowledge or heal their shame and negativity.

They do not like or accept their shadow. Their fear and shame keep their mask on and their shadow hidden. Yet, deep inside they may feel insecure and afraid. They may feel a deep, dark, unworthiness and be terrified that it will be uncovered or exposed.

Behind their fear of exposure is the belief that if their shadow were seen, they would be humiliated, rejected or even punished. This fear is so great that some people would rather die than have their dark secrets exposed.

Integrating Shadow and Persona

Healing requires the integration of shadow and mask, light and dark, conscious and unconscious within your psyche. This results in wholeness.

Neither the shadow nor the persona tells the whole truth about you. To find the truth you must integrate dark and light within your psyche. That is how you become real. You look at your strengths and weaknesses. You see both the confident adult and the scared little kid. By integrating dark and light, conscious and unconscious, good and bad, you begin to heal your divided psyche.

The division of the psyche into shadow and persona creates a kind of schizophrenia or split within your consciousness, which is then projected outward in your relationships. Healing requires that you heal that split/division within.

When you are at peace with your shadow, peace in your relationships and in your world becomes a real possibility. Inner wholeness — the redemption of the shadow from the darkness of the unconscious — thus becomes the prerequisite for the healing of our individual and collective human consciousness.

Opening Pandora's Box

Meeting your shadow is like opening Pandora's box. All kinds of unexpected things come tumbling out. It is really the beginning of the descent into the underworld to reclaim and redeem the rejected aspects of yourself. In this process, your unconscious is made conscious. Light is brought to the darkness.

This work is not about trying to get rid of fear and shame — because what you resist persists and intensifies — but about bringing your fear and shame into your conscious awareness.

When you bring light to the darkness, the darkness is illumined. When you become conscious of your fear and shame, their destructive power is diffused. When you learn to see and hold your fear and shame compassionately, you begin to embrace the angry little kid inside who does not feel loved.

Once you have awareness (light), you can bring compassion (love). That is what this work asks of you — to bring light and love, awareness and compassion — first to yourself and then to others.

Becoming aware of your shadow requires courage and compassion. You need courage to look at the parts of yourself that you don't like. You also need compassion. Otherwise you will look with judgment and that will just deepen your shame.

Your goal here is to see without judgment. So, as your fears and judgments arise, learn to hold them gently, without buying into them. Bring acceptance and love to all of the unhealed aspects of your consciousness. Realize that beneath all the negativity in your psyche is a wound that needs to be healed and know that you are taking the first step in healing it. Notice when others trigger you and ask yourself if you are seeing in them some shadow qualities that you don't want to accept in yourself. Be courageous but also be gentle with yourself and others.

Important Questions to Ask Yourself

> What do I refuse to love or accept about myself?

> What positive or negative qualities do I project onto others but have difficulty seeing in myself?

> What are my biggest fears?

> What is my deepest shame (as a child, an adolescent and an adult)?

> What are my biggest judgments of others?

> Who are the people who trigger me the most?

> What do these people show me about my shadow?

> What shadow qualities have I learned to love and accept?

> What shadow qualities are coming up right now to be integrated?

∼

Connect with Your Core Self

GOAL

Find the connection to love in your heart.

Real Happiness Roadmap
PHASE ONE

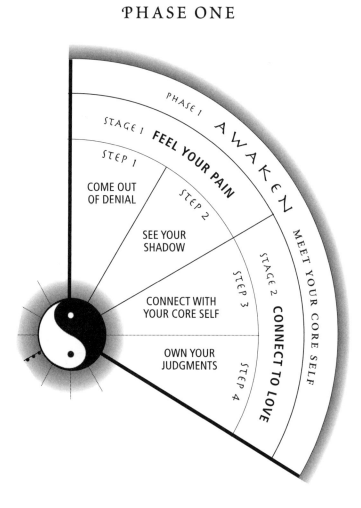

PHASE 1 AWAKEN

STAGE 1 **FEEL YOUR PAIN**

STEP 1

COME OUT
OF DENIAL

STEP 2

SEE YOUR
SHADOW

MEET YOUR CORE SELF

STAGE 2

STEP 3

CONNECT WITH
YOUR CORE SELF

CONNECT TO LOVE

OWN YOUR
JUDGMENTS

STEP 4

STRATEGY:

Enter the silence and accept your life as it is.

The Spiritual Dimension of the Core Self

The Core Self is the connection point between your divine origin and your human incarnation. It is the divine spark or essence that you bring with you into this embodiment. Your existential worth and dignity is to be found here.

The Core Self is about being, not about doing. This is the place of peace, the resting place of universal love within your consciousness. It has many names and is spoken of in many traditions

The Core Self is eternal, consistent, unchangeable. Some say it is not born and does not die because it exists beyond the vicissitudes of this world.

The Light Behind the Shadow

The Core Self is the innocent part of you that lies behind your shadow. It cannot be seen unless you look with love and acceptance. Everyone has a Core Self, but few people are in touch with it. That is because they have not yet learned to look with love and acceptance.

The Core Self is whole and complete. There is nothing lacking in it. There is nothing in it that needs to be changed or fixed. The Core Self contains all the gifts and talents you possess, in their potential. It is the blueprint you are born with. Connecting with the Core Self creates a pathway for the integration of the shadow and the restoration of wholeness in the psyche. When you are connected to your Core Self, you are connected to all that is. You live in relationship to your Source or higher power.

The Core Self exists in a state of consciousness in which there are no wounds. When we rest in the Core Self, we know that we are loved and worthy of love. There is no sense of inadequacy or self-judgment there. This is the place of unconditional love where we feel connected to everything and everyone in our experience. We feel a blissful connection to all that is.

We lose this sense of connection to the Core Self at an early age. When our needs are not met, when we are criticized or judged, we feel that there is something wrong with us. We feel inadequate, less than, unworthy. This is our personal "fall from grace." It is the moment when we lose awareness of our innocence and take on the mantle of fear and shame. Gradually, this becomes our "normal" state of consciousness. Our vibration slows down and we sink into the drama of the world, where shame and blame are commonplace.

Awareness of our connection with all that is, the Source of love, diminishes and attenuates. We have moments when we feel connected, but these are few and far between. We become invested in the world and caught up in our struggle for self-worth. We spend our lives running away from pain and trying to prove ourselves worthy of love. Yet pain follow us wherever we go, and no matter how much love we experience we still feel unworthy of it, or afraid of losing it.

To reestablish the connection to our Core Self is the goal of all spiritual practice. It is also a necessity for real healing to take place. The wounded child cannot heal himself, because he feels unworthy and has no love to bring. Someone must connect to the Source of love within and become the bringer of love to the child. This someone is you.

You are the bringer of love to your own experience. Unless you bring love to yourself, you cannot heal. You cannot experience peace in this life.

That is why this step is essential before you move on in this curriculum. You must discover the light behind your own shadow. You must come out of your head and into your heart so that you can connect with the Source of love within.

Identification with the Shadow

Only when you bring love and light can you integrate the shadow. Otherwise, you may get scared by your shadow and put your mask back on, or you may identify with your shadow and think you are bad, dark and unredeemable. When you see only your dark side you forget about your bright side.

This happens when you look at your shadow without compassion. So the goal is to see your shadow — to know that there is unconscious material that must be integrated —without identifying with it. Otherwise you may see yourself or others as evil. You may see only the devils and lose sight of the angels.

Dark and light must be accepted on equal terms for integration to take place. Darkness reaches for the light and light penetrates the darkness. Fear reaches for love and love comforts and eases the fear. Integration begins to happen. Yin and Yang, male and female, high and low, light and darkness commingle. This is an act of psychological transformation that leads to a state of unconditional acceptance and love of self and others. It is essentially blissful.

This work asks us to do two very important, but apparently opposite things. It asks us to come out of denial and come face to face with the shadow. And it asks us to see the shadow compassionately, without identifying with it. When we can see the shadow with compassion, when we can bring love to the wounded child within, genuine transformation begins. Healing energies are set into motion and go to work to bring our entire consciousness into the vibration of love.

Core Self and Inner Child Work

The Core Self is your energetic connection to love. It connects you heart to heart with other people. When you abide in the Core Self, you are incapable of judgment. You cannot think or act in a way that is hurtful to yourself or others.

Shadow work simply cannot be done without a strong connection to the Core Self and the Source of love within. There is too much of a tendency to become lost in the object and to forget to be the compassionate witness.

When you look at your fears and buy into them you make them real. You become what you are afraid of. And that is a scary proposition.

To keep your sanity, there must be a distance between you and what you see. Otherwise you many believe that what you see is what you are or what someone else is. The truth is that what you see is often seen through your own judgments and fears, so you do not see what is. You see a limited or distorted picture of reality.

The job of the witness is to see without judgment, to see and release the blocks to love one by one, as they arise. So as judgments come up, he observes them compassionately. He knows that they are not true, and so he does not try to hold onto them or justify them. He does not make the one he judges wrong or bad. He does not make himself wrong or bad for judging. He sees his judgments without identifying with them, and so he does not make them real.

The witness steps back and looks at the content of his own consciousness. He sees how his judgments and fears color his experience of reality. He sees that they are a big drama that he can buy into or not. He sees that when he buys into the drama, more drama arises. And he sees that when he no longer buys into it he begins to see what is more clearly and peacefully.

The witness looks at the contents of consciousness and removes the blocks to love. When his heart shuts down, he realizes that his muscles have contracted and that fear is coming up. He learns to take a breath and breathe with his fear. He rides out the wave of fear until it breaks and falls away.

As he does this, he begins to fall into his heart. He begins to sink down beneath the layer of consciousness permeated by fear. He moves beyond shame and blame into a quiet place. He begins to feel energy in his heart as he realizes that he is okay the way he is. Others are okay the way they are. Life is acceptable just the way it is in this moment.

The more he accepts, the more the energy intensifies in his heart chakra and begins to move throughout his body. He begins to feel the energy of love as a palpable presence, an intense vibration, a kind of burning bush in his heart, the heat of which extends into his hands and feet, his throat and his belly, his root and his crown. Gradually, love permeates and inhabits his whole body and he is filled with light and grace.

As you learn to sit in the silence and sink into your essence, your heart of hearts, you encounter the one who is innocent, whole and complete. You meet the one who lives in acceptance and bliss. That one is within you. S/he is the one you truly are when you leave the drama of the world behind.

Truth and Illusion

The Core Self is the light behind the shadow. When we look compassionately at the shadow, we realize it is all illusion. It is a construction of our shame and our fear. It is not ultimately real. What is ultimately real is what stands behind it.

Until now, the light has been hidden behind the shadow. But when we meet the shadow without fear, we can see the light behind it.

Beneath your guilt is your innocence. The latter is real. The former is not.

Guilt occurs only when you lose sight of your innocence and buy into someone else's story about you. That story is not true, not for you nor for him. When you know that, you don't take the story on. You say, "That's an interesting story, but I don't think it's true for me."

You see that the shadow arises when we believe something that is not true about us or another. It is not ultimately real. But it seems to be real when most people believe it and act according to their beliefs.

That is why it is so hard to challenge the dominant reality of the world that perpetuates shame and blame. It seems to be real enough. One person hurts another and the other hurts him back. Each is just proving out his belief. The strange thing is that he can prove out his belief and it can still be completely wrong and delusional.

Each one of us will have an experience of the world that conforms to his beliefs about himself and others. This experience may be painful, but it still may be difficult to challenge. People think "this is just the way it is." But in truth it is just the way "they perceive it to be."

Whatever a person perceives seems "real enough" to him. He identifies with what he perceives, accepts it as truth, and lives his life according to that truth. But that truth might not lead him out of suffering. It might not help him to live a happy and fulfilled life. Indeed, it may be the primary cause of his suffering. Yet, until his pain is very great, he may not question what he believes to be true. He may not know that he has the power to liberate himself, just as he had the power to put himself in prison.

Sooner or later, the pain gets too much to bear. That's when we get on our knees and ask for help. That's when we begin to question our assumptions and open up to looking at things differently so that we can make different choices.

The False Self will self-destruct sooner or later. Humpty Dumpty will fall off the wall and smash into thousands of pieces. The world that we built in fear and shame will shatter when we can no longer bear the pain. And then everything will change.

When the shadow integrates, nothing can block the light of the Core Self. It shines forth unfettered and free, illuminating all the worlds and levels of manifest existence. There is no place where its light cannot reach. There is no place that cannot be touched by its love.

That is why we do this work. To sink into our essence. To bring our darkness to light and to become the light that we are, so that we can go forth and fulfill our creative purpose and give our gifts to the world.

Your Core Self is innocent, whole and complete. It is your essence. It is the shining one you are when your heart is open to love and you know that you and everyone else is worthy of acceptance and love.

The Core Self, the False Self and the True Self

When you try to act without a connection to your Core Self, all that you create is wound-driven. Every attempt to act without this connection is simply wrongdoing. It leads to wrong relationship, wrong livelihood and all other expressions of self-betrayal. These are the activities of the False Self.

When you meet and align with the Core Self everything you do is congruent with it. As a result, you spontaneously honor self and other. This leads to right action, right livelihood, right relationship. These are the activities of the True Self.

The False Self betrays the Core Self. The True Self honors the Core Self. Indeed it can be said that while the Core Self is not in the world, the True Self is the engine of its expression in this world.

Making Time for Self-Communion

To be a light-bearer, you must have the courage to enter the dark tunnel of your shame and pain and reclaim your innocence. You must learn to hold your fears gently and bring love to all the wounded places in yourself.

Your most important practice is to take time in silence each day to connect to your Core Self and the presence of love in your heart. You connect to your Core Self by letting go of your judgments, accepting your life experience just as it is, and by feeling gratitude for all the gifts you have received.

When you feel connected to love, you sink into your essence and know it deeply and without question. You reclaim your innocence and bring love to all the wounded places in yourself. Then you can emerge from the darkness holding the light, first for yourself, and then for others.

The choice to connect with your Core Self and to learn to trust it is the most important decision you will make. Making time and space for this connection may require a reordering of your priorities in life.

Important Questions to Ask Yourself

> When I am connected to my Core Self, do I notice that shame and blame fall away and I see my innocence and that of others?

> What was my most profound experience or encounter with my Core Self and how did it change my life?

> When did I feel most disconnected from my Core Self and most out of alignment with the truth of my being?

> To what extent am I looking for answers outside of myself vs. finding the light and the connection to love within?

> Do I take time each day to enter the silence and connect with my Core Self?

4

~

Own Your Judgments

GOAL

Stop projecting your pain onto others.

STRATEGY

Learn to bring love to the wounded part of you
that judges and finds fault with others.

Judgments Lead to Attack

Our judgments of others lead to one form of attack or another. They are the beginning of trespass. When we judge another person, we attempt to make something stick to him or her that belongs to us. If we judge another person as lazy, it is usually because we are lazy or are afraid of being seen as lazy. If laziness was not our issue, if we were not criticized for it by our parents and other authority figures, if we did not feel shame about it, or fear being punished for it, we would not have an antenna that picks up laziness in others. We see in others what we are afraid to see in ourselves.

That way instead of feeling our shame, we shame others. We say about our brother in law, "He's a lazy slob. He hasn't had a job in three years." And that may be true about him, but it may also be true about us. We think that by making it be about him, we take ourselves off the hook. It becomes his problem, not ours. But that is just wishful thinking. Shaming or blaming him does not make our shame go away. It just reinforces it. There's no way out of the blame game, except to heal our shame and stop blaming others.

Once one person attacks another, it isn't long before the other person fights back. Before long, someone ups the ante and throws a punch, or picks up a gun. Before you know it someone is hurt or dead. Words escalate into deeds. Fear becomes attack. Shame becomes humiliation.

All of this starts with a single judgment made by a person who does not feel loved or worthy. Instead of feeling his shame and working to heal it, he tries to shame someone else. He projects his issue onto his coworker or his partner.

It is not a mystery that domestic crimes are so prevalent in society. We tend to attack the people we hang out with. They are the ones who trigger us best because they know how to get under our skin.

Jesus told us that we had to look not just at our acts, but at our thoughts too. Acts begin as thoughts. If we don't bring awareness and healing at the thought stage, it will be harder after the actions have been taken.

That is why we all need to be vigilant for our thoughts before they become words and for our words before they become actions. In this sense, owning our judgments becomes the first step in ending the cycle of violence where it begins, in our own hearts and minds.

Owning Your Judgments

In Step Four you are asked to understand that your judgments belong to you, not to anyone else. Instead of projecting your shadow onto others you are asked to see the unworthiness behind your judgments and bring love to the wounded and unworthy parts of yourself.

By taking responsibility for the judgment, you are able to bring correction and forgiveness. You are able to hear and respond to the call for love from the wounded child within yourself.

The goal here is not for you to stop having judgments — that is an unrealistic expectation — but simply for you to be aware of the judgments that arise in your mind. We are asking you to see them, correct them, and forgive them.

Your judgments of others reflect back to you where your real issues of self-worth lie. When you judge another person, you project some aspect of yourself onto someone else. That is why your judgments are about you, not about someone else. Your judgments about others offer you an opportunity to look at the unloved/unaccepted aspects of yourself and bring love and acceptance to them. That's why recognizing your judgments can be the key toward healing your wounds.

None of your judgments are justified. They are all unjustified and untrue. Your attempt to justify your judgments is an exercise in denial and a refusal to take responsibility for your thoughts, words, and actions.

When you acknowledge your judgments (know that they are about you and not about anyone else) you stop projecting. Awareness and responsibility stop projection in its tracks.

When you own your judgments and bring love and acceptance to the aspect of self that feels unworthy, you begin to integrate your shadow. You move toward unity and wholeness.

Forgiveness and Correction

Forgiveness involves awareness and correction. First you see and correct your judgments and then you forgive yourself for making them. The correction to each judgment is "I see that this is not about you. It is about me." That is what it means to own the judgment and take it back. Then you ask, "Where is the wound behind this judgment? How is the other person reflecting something that is painful to me?"

If you were feeling safe and secure right now you would not be judging. So you ask, "How am I feeling scared or unsafe? Where do I need to bring love and acceptance to myself?"

This process of awareness, correction and forgiveness is essential if you are going to learn to take responsibility for your thoughts, words and actions. Since we all project, since we all judge, we must all learn to own our judgments so that we can correct them and forgive ourselves and others. This becomes a daily and even a moment-to-moment practice.

To correct and forgive is to heal, atone and reconnect with your Core Self and the Core Self in others. That is what it means to be truly responsible for your thoughts, words and deeds.

Projection: The Futile Attempt to Escape Your Shadow

Your judgments are the way that you unconsciously project your shadow onto others. Because you don't want to look at your shadow, you try to get rid of it by projecting it outward. However, this strategy is completely ineffective. When you judge others, they don't like it. They don't accept your judgments and usually judge you back. You attack them and they attack you. You don't succeed in getting rid of your self-judgment. You merely externalize it so that you get to look at it.

In the end you come face to face with all of the fear and

shame reflected back to you through others. Projection is just a big mirror that shows you what you don't want to look at. In other words, you cannot escape your shadow. You have to look at it. You have to encounter your wound.

Holding onto Your Judgments

None of your judgments is justified. This needs to be understood and accepted. Otherwise, you will live in denial.

When you try to justify your judgments you hold onto them. Only when you realize that your judgments are untrue and unjustified, can you let them go.

Holding onto your judgments reinforces the division in your psyche between persona and shadow. That means that you do not heal and experience your wholeness. Your shadow remains un-integrated.

Taking Responsibility

Step Four is all about taking responsibility for the contents of your consciousness. Your judgments belong to you, not to anyone else. You are asked to see and own your judgments as they come up, see the unworthiness behind them, and bring love to the wounded child within.

- First you take others off the hook. You see the judgment. Then you own it and refrain from projecting it onto someone else.

- Second you take yourself off the hook. You see your judgment as a call for love and acceptance, and you learn to bring love to the unworthy and wounded parts of yourself.

By taking responsibility for the judgment, you are able to bring correction and forgiveness. And you are able to hear and respond to the call for love from the wounded child within yourself.

Experiential Practice for Step Four

Notice the judgments that you make about others. Many people think that judgments are bad and we should make them go away. But I can tell you from experience that this strategy doesn't work. If you try to make your judgments go away, they will either intensify, or they will go underground.

When judgments "go underground" they drop out of your awareness. It doesn't mean that you have stopped judging. It just means that you are not aware of your judgments. So you walk around pretending that you don't have any judgments when you have hundreds of them.

So take a deep breath and start looking at the contents of your consciousness. Don't be afraid to see all the ways that you feel "less than" or "more than" others. I assure you: you aren't the only one who is feeling like this.

The more you observe your judgments, the more you begin to see how many layers of judgment there are in your consciousness. First you judge, and then you judge your judgment. You beat yourself up for being judgmental, and so the downward spiral of judgment continues. You have to catch this spiral somewhere. At some point you have to say, "Okay. I see I'm judging. It's okay. It's no big deal. We all do it. My job is just to be aware of my judgments and hold them compassionately."

If you stay with this process of observing your judgments,

you begin to ask, "What's behind this judgment?" Invariably you will find it is some form of shame or fear inside of you.

Now you are coming closer to your wound. And that is what needs to be healed. It's not the judgment that you need to focus on — because all judgments of others or yourself are untrue and unjustified — it's the wound that causes the judgment. It is the pain that you are attempting to externalize and project outward onto others.

Behind your pain and discomfort is a need for some love and acceptance. You can realize that and give yourself some love right now. This brings the judgment trail to its end. It cancels your projection of your shame and unworthiness onto others. Instead, you are able to confront these feelings directly.

Steps to Follow in Owning Your Judgments

Here are the steps to follow in owning your judgments.

1. Become aware of your judgments.

2. Don't beat yourself up for having judgments.

3. Realize that your judgment is not accurate and can't be justified.

4. Own the judgment. Understand that it's ultimately about you, not about the other person.

5. See that your judgment of yourself is not true either.

6. See the fear or feeling of unworthiness behind the judgment.

7. Hold your fear with love and compassion.

If you are able to go through this whole process, you will not only become aware of your judgments, you will also be able to release them. In the process, you will tune into some of your childhood wounds and begin to bring healing to yourself and integration to your psyche. Most importantly, you will begin to learn how to hold your fears in a loving and compassionate way. This is a foundational spiritual practice.

Important Questions to Ask Yourself

> Who are the three people I judge the most and what are my judgments about them? (Exaggerate your judgments if necessary to articulate them clearly.)

> Who do I put up on a pedestal? Who do I look down on? (Remember judgments can be positive or negative. You can see others as more or less worthy than you.)

> How can I take these people off the hook and make this be about me, not about them?

> By looking at what I project (don't like or accept about others), can I see mirrored back to me aspects of myself that I have trouble liking or accepting?

> Can I look behind the judgment and see how I feel scared or unsafe?

> Can I feel the pain or discomfort behind the judgment and tune into the wounded child within who needs my reassurance and love?

TRANSITION TO PHASE TWO

~

Bringing Light and Love to the Shadowy Realm

In order to move successfully to Phase Two of this healing process, you need to understand that you are the bringer of love to your own experience. That is your job and your responsibility.

You cannot rely on anyone else to do this for you. You have to learn how to accept and bless yourself. If you try to heal your Core Wound without establishing your connection to love, you will fail. It will be like entering a dark cave without bringing the light with you. You will not be able to navigate the terrain of the shadow unless you bring the light with you as you descend underground.

Despite the warnings, some people try to take the journey before they are ready. They enter the shadowy world and get stuck or lost. They blame themselves and others. They deepen their pain and their shame. They cannot find their way forward, nor can they easily retrace their steps. Simply put, they get stuck in their pain. They do not move through it. That is both tragic and unnecessary.

Please make a solid connection to the Source of love in your heart before you attempt to investigate your wound and the shame around it. Practice seeing the light behind the shadow. Practice looking at your judgments with compassion. Learn to become a bringer of love to your own experience. Then you can enter the dark tunnel of your pain carrying the light of awareness and the blessing of love.

If you are having difficulty connecting to love, you may not be ready to move into Phase Two of this work. Take some time to learn to open your heart. Join an *Affinity Group* or attend a *Phase One Real Happiness Intensive* so that you can receive the support of others as you move into your healing journey.

PART TWO

Healing

Real Happiness Roadmap
PHASE TWO

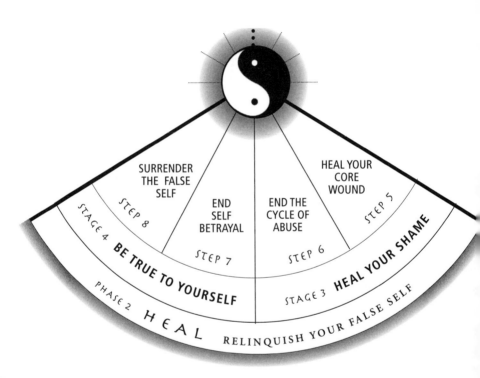

SURRENDER
THE FALSE
SELF

HEAL YOUR
CORE
WOUND

END
SELF
BETRAYAL

END THE
CYCLE OF
ABUSE

STAGE 4   STEP 8   STEP 7   STEP 6   STEP 5

BE TRUE TO YOURSELF

STAGE 3   HEAL YOUR SHAME

PHASE 2   HEAL   RELINQUISH YOUR FALSE SELF

Heal Your Core Wound

GOAL

Identify your mommy/daddy wound,
your core belief, and your reactive behavior pattern.

STRATEGY:

Connect with the wounded child within.

Mommy and Daddy Wounds

Each of us has a mommy wound and/or a daddy wound. A mommy wound involves too much, too little, or inappropriate attention from Mommy. A daddy wound involves too much, too little, or inappropriate attention from Daddy.

People with mommy wounds have a hard time learning to love and accept themselves and others. Relationships are challenging for them and bring most of their lessons. They do not easily experience intimacy with others.

People with daddy wounds have a hard time being successful in the world. They often struggle in their careers and have difficulty supporting themselves and making a living. They often lack self-confidence and do not believe in themselves. They frequently do not take the time to develop the skills they need to be successful.

A good relationship with Mommy bodes well for success in relationships. A good relationship with Daddy bodes well for success in career.

Types of Core Wounds

Your core wound may be a mommy wound, a daddy wound, or a combination of both. For example, abandonment is a core wound. You can be abandoned by Mommy or Daddy or by both of them.

Abandonment can be physical or mental/emotional. It may include the death or illness of one or both parents or their unavailability because of divorce, active military service, addiction to drugs or alcohol, postpartum depression or another mental condition.

Betrayal is another type of core wound. Betrayal occurs when trust is established and then destroyed. It happens when there is a sudden ambivalence or instability in the attention of parents or caretakers. It may happen when a sibling dies and a parent emotionally disconnects from the surviving child. It can happen when the adult withdraws emotionally due to an unexpected trauma or physical or mental illness. It happens when a parent or caretaker abuses a child (and this includes physical, sexual, emotional, or ritual abuse). It happens when there is incest or other inappropriate behavior with siblings or other family members. The wound is exacerbated if the parent knew about the abuse and did nothing to protect the child.

Another wound is imprisonment/confinement. It happens when parents lock up, overly control or limit the freedom of a child. Lack of limits can also be a wound. In this case parents/caretakers do not pay adequate attention to the child and allow him or her an unsafe amount of freedom or responsibility. Both over-protection and lack of protection can be wounds.

Stolen childhood is yet another wound. This occurs when parents/caretakers are ill or emotionally unavailable and the child is forced to play the role of parent and takes on adult responsibilities before s/he has grown up.

Repeated humiliation, criticism, shaming, and blaming by parents/significant others is another common core wound. Other core wounds can result from

- Pampering, spoiling, low expectations, overprotection

- Danger/lack of safety (physical or emotional)

- Guilt, false responsibility (for a parent or sibling's death or illness)

- Birth trauma, birth defects, premature birth, serious childhood illness

- Not being wanted, unplanned pregnancy

- Rejection by a parent

- Persecution by siblings

As you read through the list, other wounds may occur to you. It doesn't have to be on this list to be a core wound. When you tune into your childhood, you know what you experienced as most hurtful. You know what made you feel most afraid or ashamed. You know in what way you received too much, too little, or inappropriate attention from one or both of your parents, caretakers, siblings or significant others in your life.

Try to spend some time journaling about this. See if you can identify your core wound and understand how it has impacted your life.

Core Beliefs

All core wounds lead directly to a core belief about yourself. For example if Mommy was ill when you were seven years old and you were asked to be her caretaker, you might grow up with one of these core beliefs:

• I have to take care of others to get their love.

• My needs don't matter.

On the other hand, if your parents pushed you to perform and be successful at school, in sports, or in beauty contests, you might grow up with one of these core beliefs:

• I am stronger, smarter, or more beautiful than others.

• If I am not stronger, smarter, or more beautiful than others I won't be loved.

Your core belief is created out of the shame or unworthiness attached to your core wound. In both of the above examples the shame/unworthiness is the internalized message "I am not good enough as I am. I will only be good enough if I show up the way that Mommy or Daddy want me to (as the caretaker, the good little girl or boy, the beauty queen, star student or athlete)."

All core beliefs can be summed up by the overall belief "I am not worthy of love," or (another version of the same thing) "I have to jump through hoops to be worthy of love."

Once your core belief is formed, you carry it unconsciously through your life. Even after you leave home you act in a way that is consistent with your core belief. If you learn to be the caretaker and hold the belief "My needs don't matter," it is very likely that you will marry a spouse that you have to take care of. It is not until you heal your wound and the belief attached to it that you are able to conclude that "my needs matter" and insist on creating a relationship with someone who can take care of himself or herself.

Once you heal your mommy or daddy wound, you no longer have to marry Mommy or Daddy. But until you heal that wound, you will operate with the belief that "my needs don't matter" or "I have to take care of others to be loved," and you will continue to marry Mommy or Daddy over and over again. This is why after getting divorced, you marry someone just like your former husband or wife. You marry just another version of Mommy or Daddy because you have not healed your wound and changed the core belief attached to it.

Of course there are as many core beliefs as there are core wounds. Here are a few core beliefs that you might recognize:

- Nothing I do is good enough.

- It's my fault. I am to blame.

- I'm a bad or evil person (or I would not have been beaten/ sexually abused).

- If I ask for what I need, I will be abandoned

- If I am powerful, I won't be loved. I must play small and hold myself back.

- I am a failure. I will never amount to anything.

- I am stupid. Others are smarter than I am.

- I have to be smarter than others to be loved.

- I have to be thin. If I am fat I won't be loved.

- I am weak or sickly. If I heal, I won't be loved.

- The world is not a safe place. If I take a risk, I will be hurt.

- I show up for others, but no one shows up for me.

- I can't do it by myself. I need someone to do it for me.

- I have to do it by myself. No one else can help.

- My ideas/opinion do not matter.

- When I trust the universe, I get smashed.

- I have to be silent/invisible. If I am seen and heard, I will be rejected.

As you read the above list, you may think of other beliefs that you internalized at an early age. Make some notes in your journal about these beliefs. They may be driving your life at an unconscious level. Becoming conscious of them is very important.

Reactive Behavior Patterns

Your reactive behavior pattern is usually triggered by people who confirm your core belief about yourself. For example, if you believe that "I must be skinny in order to get love and attention" and someone says "You're a bit chubby," you are likely to be triggered. Your shame about carrying too much weight and your fear of rejection are brought up. You believe you must be skinny to be loved, so in your eyes they are judging you to be ugly and unlovable, even if that was not what they were trying to convey to you. On the other hand, maybe they are judging you because they have the same core belief and they are projecting it onto you. This happens a lot.

However, even if they are projecting, they are not responsible for the pain and distress that come up for you. That was already there before they crossed your path. Their judgment/trespass on you just gives you an opportunity to look at your core wound and core belief and begin to heal them.

Here's another example. Let's say your mom and dad are both university professors and they value logic and left-brain intelligence. You and your brother are both brought up to believe that you won't be loved and accepted unless you excel in math or science. Your brother is good at these things. You are not. You are good at music and art, neither of which your parents value. So your brother gets all the praise and kudos. You get very little understanding or support. Your gifts are not encouraged. So you begin to internalize the message "I'm not smart like my brother. I won't amount to very much."

What do you do with the core belief? How does it run your life? You might just give up on yourself very early in life and set very low expectations of yourself. On the other hand, you might try to defy the odds and go to engineering school in the hopes of pleasing Mom and Dad. You might be absolutely miserable there but force yourself to stay because it's the only way to get the approval you so desperately want.

Then along comes your friend Marc who is a whiz at calculus, and when the two of you are doing your homework together, he says, "You know, you really aren't very good at this...maybe you should consider a different major." He is just trying to be helpful, and you know he is right, but his comment gets under your skin and you react to it. So you get mad at Marc and avoid seeing him for the rest of the semester.

Let's look at your wound, your core belief and your reactive behavior pattern so we can see the whole picture.

- Your wound: mental and emotional abandonment, lack of encouragement and support from both parents, especially from Daddy.

- Your belief: "I will not be loved unless I am smart (like my brother)."

- My brother gets the love. He's Daddy's favorite. I can't follow my heart and express my gifts or I won't be loved."

- Reactive Behavior: Run away/withdraw from Marc when he shows up as the *Whiz Kid* (your brother) and triggers your core belief.

Three Types of Reactive Behavior Patterns

There are three types of reactive behavior patterns:

- Fight: You attack others back.

- Flight: You run away from others.

- Hide: You stay but withdraw/shut down emotionally.

These are the ways you react when you are triggered by other people. You may have one, two or all three of these patterns. Often, you copy the ones your parents had.

It is important to get clear on which patterns you have and where you learned them. Take some time to reflect on this in your journal. It is important.

Why Affirmations Don't Reverse our Core Beliefs

There are many new age pundits who suggest that you can change your core belief at will. You can go from being a loser to a winner just by saying "I am a winner" over and over in your mind.

Now, I don't mean to suggest that there is no power in positive thinking. There is, and I encourage you to be as positive as you can be. But many new age ideas are one-dimensional and have no grasp of the power of the shadow to shape our lives. They ignore the unconscious, more primitive aspect of the psyche and, as such, have no transformative power. They are ineffective in helping us heal at depth and get our lives on track.

Suppose, for example, that you are a woman who consciously holds the belief "I am a child of God" and repeats that constantly as an affirmation in your life. As a child, your father sexually abused you and you went on to become a sexual object for a series of men believing you would be loved only if you had sex with them. Of course, that strategy did not work, and every time a man left you behind, your shame and humiliation deepened.

If you are honest about how that little girl inside you feels — the girl who never grew up emotionally or gained any confidence in or respect for herself as a woman — you would realize that she would not say, "I feel like a child of God." She would say something like, "I suck. I hate myself and nobody will ever really love me." And you know what? She would be telling the truth. That's how she really feels.

So you can walk around wearing your spiritual mask saying "I am a child of God," but it isn't going to help the little girl heal. It isn't going to help her grow up and gain confidence and respect so that she can attract a good relationship with a man. All it is going to do is set her up, over and over again, for pain and disappointment.

When the affirmation "I am a child of God" does not work, you are going to feel like a failure. You are going to reinforce your shame and unworthiness and continue to believe that you can never do anything right.

That's when you will be ready to put the affirmation aside for a while and come and do your real healing. Unless you identify your wound, your core belief and your reactive behavior pattern, you cannot begin to heal at depth and come into your true power and purpose as a human being.

You are a child of God. That is the truth. But you have to do your emotional healing to begin to believe it. And until you believe it, from the inside out, it won't really be true for you.

Ancestral Wounds: Understanding the Chain of Abuse

It is a fact of life that our parents pass their wounds/beliefs/reactive behavior patterns onto us, and we pass our wounds/beliefs/reactive behavior patterns onto our children. This pattern continues until someone in the family becomes conscious of the wound and heals it.

As adults we frequently marry someone just like the parent who wounded us the most. If it was Mommy, we marry Mommy. If it was Daddy, we marry Daddy. That way we get another chance to heal our mommy and daddy wound.

However, there is another way that the wound can be passed down. If we have a mommy wound, but Mommy is too scary, we may marry Daddy instead, because he is less scary to us. So in this case we become Mommy and marry Daddy. On the other hand, if we have a daddy wound and Daddy is too scary, we may marry Mommy instead. In this case, we become Daddy and marry Mommy.

Needless to say, all of this happens regardless of the whether the Mommy or Daddy we marry is male or female. Sometimes a woman marries a man who is Mommy and a man marries a woman who is Daddy. This makes it a little difficult to sort out. But a little introspection usually brings clarity.

If you are old enough to have children or grandchildren, you can see how these patterns continue in your family. You can trace the wound/belief/reactive behavior down through the generations.

On the other hand, please take care not to go into your head around this process. Our goal here is our own emotional healing and empowerment, not a precise intellectual understanding of the patterns. Sometimes intellectualizing this material prevents us from feeling it and healing it. So a word here to the wise: "Heal it first; study it later."

Important Questions to Ask Yourself

> What is my mommy wound?

> What is my daddy wound?

> Did my wound come from my siblings or other family members or from someone outside my family?

> Was my wound an event or circumstance like an accident or serious illness?

> What is my core belief? What judgments about me did I internalize growing up?

> Did my core belief come from Mommy, Daddy, or from both?

> How does my core belief drive my life unconsciously? How has it influenced the major decisions/choices I have made?

> What is/are my reactive behavior pattern(s)?

> Did I learn it from Mommy, from Daddy, or from both?

> Did I marry Mommy or Daddy?

> Did I become Mommy and marry Daddy?

> Did I become Daddy and marry Mommy?

> Did this pattern change in my subsequent marriages/relationships?

6

End the Cycle of Abuse

GOAL

See and end the patterns of victimization.

STRATEGY:

Forgive yourself and others.

Victims and Victimizers

As you look at the wounds you have given and received, it is important to understand the ways that you have shown up as a victim or as a victimizer. Most of us show up at one time or another in both roles.

Moreover, victims tend to become victimizers. Those who were beaten or sexually abused as children often abuse their own children or the children of others. We do to others what has been done to us. There is no end to the chain of abuse as long as we keep it going. Our choice is always to stop it here and now.

How to End the Chain of Abuse

To end the chain of abuse we must forgive our abusers and ourselves and we must refuse to show up anymore as either a victim or a victimizer. That means learning to forgive our parents for trespassing against us and learning to forgive ourselves for not standing up to them or to anyone else who has victimized us. If we have become victimizers of others, we must understand how we were victims first and bring healing and compassion to our wounds. Then we must also seek the understanding and forgiveness of those we have hurt, whether they be parents, siblings, spouses or children.

Forgiveness is a process that happens in layers and often

takes years. You cannot rush the process or force yourself to forgive before you are ready. While forgiving others and forgiving ourselves are two sides of the same coin, the latter is often the more difficult aspect of the process.

Self-forgiveness is possible even if others do not forgive you. Even if others forgive you, you might not forgive yourself. As a general rule, your capacity to forgive others depends on your willingness to forgive yourself. It is also true that your capacity to forgive yourself depends to some extent on your willingness to forgive others.

Seven Steps in the Forgiveness Process

Here are seven steps that will help you to forgive yourself and others. They will help you to cover all the bases. But do be patient with the process. It does not happen over night. Often it takes years. Sometimes it even takes generations.

1. Accept What Happened

You can't pretend that it didn't happen. You can't go back and undo it. You can't fix it or change it. You just have to accept that it happened and it is therefore part of your life. Acceptance sometimes takes a while.

2. Feel Compassion for Yourself

If you have been victimized, you need to stop blaming yourself for what happened. You are not to blame. You are not bad, unworthy or unlovable. You are not dirty, ugly, stained or damaged goods. Even if you are a victimizer, you were very likely a victim at some time in your life.

3. Forgive Yourself

Regardless of whether you are a victim or a victimizer, or both, this process of self-forgiveness may take a long time. It may even take your whole life. But it is very important. You need to commit to this process if you really want to heal.

4. Feel Compassion for the Victimizer

Understand the pain of the person who wounded you and learn to feel compassion for that person. Most victimizers were victims once, and they are doing to you what was done to them. But first you may have to get in touch with and express your anger at this person. This too can take some time.

5. Forgive the Victimizer

Eventually you are going to have to forgive the other person. That does not mean that you condone his/her behavior. But you realize that the behavior was caused by his/her own pain/abuse. You also realize that not forgiving this person means that you are holding onto your bitterness, and this prevents you from moving forward in your own life.

6. Detach and Let Go

After forgiving yourself and the other person, you can detach and let go of your identity as a victim. You stop speaking or acting in a way that seeks sympathy from others or reinforces your belief that you are wounded and cannot heal. You also stop condemning the abuser/victimizer and release the person emotionally.

7. You Heal Your Wound and Release the Past

After you detach, your wound begins to heal. A scab forms over the wound. You grow new skin. You do not deny what happened, but there is no more charge on it for you. You do not condemn yourself or the other person. You learn whatever lesson you can learn from the experience and put it behind you.

Refuse to Show Up as Either a Victim or a Victimizer

As we have said before, forgiveness and correction go hand and hand. Ultimately there is no forgiveness without correction. You can't shift a negative pattern in your life unless you are willing to do your part to change it.

Forgiving the victimizer is one part of the process of healing. The other part is your commitment to stand up and say "No" to those who would abuse you. This is not about blaming you for what happened in the past. Absolutely not. You could not stand up for yourself when you were three years old and were overpowered by an adult. But you can stand up for yourself now.

When people try to impose their will on you, you can refuse to cooperate. You can tell them that you don't need their advice or their interference in your life. You can tell them that you are committed to making your own decisions now. If they don't give you the space that you are asking for, you can ask them to leave or you can leave them. You don't have to stay and take it anymore.

You heal your patterns of victimhood by taking charge of your life and setting strong, healthy boundaries with others. You forgive what happened in the past. But you resolve not to let it happen in the future. You need to work on both ends. Indeed, you cannot do one without doing the other.

If you are a victimizer, you must not only seek the forgiveness of others whom you have hurt. You must refuse to hurt anyone else. You must accept the limits that others try to set with you. You must stop trying to control them or interfere in their lives. You must learn to mind your own business and get in touch with your own pain. You became a victimizer for a reason . . . someone at some time in your life victimized you. You need to get in touch with the fear and shame around that and heal your wound so that you don't go out and victimize someone else. You must end the cycle of violence where it starts, in your own heart and mind.

Give up Shame and Blame

It is always tempting to blame our parents, spouses and others for the wounds we have suffered. We make it their fault. We cast them out of our hearts. We feel entitled to our hurt. Indeed, we hold onto it. In some cases, our wound becomes a badge of honor that we wear proudly. It helps us to get sympathy from others. It gives us the attention we are not sure that we would otherwise have.

I call this "making our identity in the wound." It is a form of attachment to the victim role that prevents us from healing. Our fear is that when we stop playing the role of the victim, others will no longer pay attention to us.

Letting go of an old identity is not easy. It is impossible as long as there is a payoff for keeping it. We are not usually willing to stop our identification until there is more pain than pay-off in it. Moreover, we are so used to playing this role, we are not sure that we have the ability or the power to stop it. Indeed, saying "No" to others who want to take care of us and making our own choices can be terrifying to us. It is easier to keep the status quo. Then we won't have to move out of our comfort zone and risk failure and humiliation.

There are two dysfunctional extremes when it comes to the process of healing the wounded child. One is that we deny our wound or we anesthetize the pain around it. In this case, we don't feel the pain and we can't heal it. The other extreme is that we become attached to our wound and make our identity in it. In that case, we become a professional victim who thrives on telling old war stories and reliving the trauma of the past.

Neither of these extremes is helpful. We don't want to deny the wound or become attached to it. We want to see it, feel it, and heal it.

Blaming our parents keeps us locked in victimhood. It may be something that happens in the early stages of our healing journey when we first begin to feel the pain of our wound. We may experience anger — even rage — that we did not know that we had. But that is Phase One of this work. We don't move into Phase Two until we stop blaming others and begin to take responsibility for our own healing.

Taking Responsibility for Your Own Healing

If we want to heal our core wound, we can't engage in blame or become permanent victims. We have to take responsibility for our wound. It belongs to us, at least for now. And we are the only ones who can heal it.

This means that we must engage in a process of forgiving ourselves and others that will take years. We must not be put off by that. Just because the journey is a long one does not mean that we cannot reach our goal.

However, we will not reach our goal if we allow ourselves to be overwhelmed by the size of the task. We begin our thousand-mile journey by taking the first step. We learn to be gentle with ourselves and with others. We put one foot in front of the other. We take it one day at a time. Gradually, we see that we have made progress. When we look back, we can barely see the place where we started.

Now we are in the middle of the desert. Going back is not possible. Now we know we have made the commitment to heal, no matter how long it takes.

Bringing Love to the Child Within

Most of us don't realize that there is a scared little kid inside who is running our lives. We don't realize it, that is, until that kid goes on the warpath. Then, we and everyone else in our lives can't help but notice.

If we want to heal our wound, we are going to have to stop abandoning the shadow aspect of ourselves. We are going to have to pick up that rejected little kid and learn to love him or her. We all need to go through a healing process in which we learn to love that scared little kid inside and reclaim our innocence.

Mommy or Daddy may have abandoned us and helped to set all this up. But, in the end, we are the ones who abandon ourselves. We have to stop doing that. We have to start showing up for the child within. We have to become the Mommy or Daddy that s/he never had.

In the process, we go from being the one who is wounded to the one who brings acceptance and love. The wounded child within does not know how to bring love. For years, we were so freaked out by him or her that we did not know how to bring love either. So the cries of the wounded child were ignored. We heard the wailing in the darkness, but we could not respond to it. We heard the call for love, but we could not answer it.

Guess what? Now we hear that call and we know that we are the only ones who can respond to it. We know that we are the bringers of love to our own experience. We feel compassion for the suffering of the little child within. We feel her pain, her anger, her grief. We are no longer put off by her screams or her tears. We reach down and wrap her in our arms. "I am here," we tell her. "I am with you now and I will not leave you. I will not abandon you anymore."

The spiritual adult and the wounded child come face to face and join together in the spirit of acceptance and love. The child begins to feel safe, to heal and spread her wings. The spiritual adult sets boundaries with others and keeps the space safe so that the little kid can gain confidence and strength.

The child is gradually re-parented and grows up feeling worthy of love. The Christ child and the wounded child become one in the manger of our hearts. As the child heals, the shadow is integrated and the light behind the shadow shines through. The True Self is born.

From the ashes of the fire of destruction, the phoenix arises and spreads its wings. Resurrection is at hand. That which has died has been reborn. If you listen, you can hear the angels dancing in heaven.

Important Questions to Ask Yourself

> Have I forgiven my mother and father?

> Have they forgiven me?

> Have I forgiven my siblings?

> Have they forgiven me?

> Have I forgiven my spouse?

> Has s/he forgiven me?

> Have I forgiven my children?

> Have they forgiven me?

> Am I withholding forgiveness from anyone?

> Who is the person I have hurt the most? Have I asked for forgiveness and made amends with this person?

> What is the biggest thing I have forgiven another person for?

> Have I forgiven myself?

> What is the biggest thing I have forgiven myself for?

> In what ways have I shown up as a victim?

> In what ways have I shown up as a victimizer?

> If I am a victim, have I taken my power back and set healthy limits with others?

> Am I attached to being a victim?

> If I am a victimizer, have I stopped crossing the boundaries of others and begun to investigate my own pain?

> Have I shopped blaming others and started to take responsibility for my own healing?

7

~

End the Patterns of Self-Betrayal

GOAL

Have the courage to be yourself.

Real Happiness Roadmap

PHASE TWO

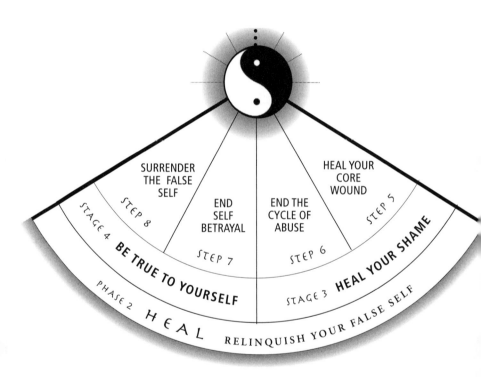

STRATEGY

Take your power back.

Patterns of Domination, Submission, Passive-Aggression, and Escape

Your reactive behavior pattern is connected to your energetic stance. You tend to be dominant or submissive in your relationships. You tend to give your power away and allow others to make decisions for you, or you tend to be controlling and to make decisions for others.

Your energetic stance sets up the way your relationships are structured at home and at work. It may limit the amount of creative freedom you have in your life. There are four basic energetic patterns: dominant, submissive, passive-aggressive, and evasive/withdrawing.

If you have a *dominant* energetic pattern you tend to make decisions for others and to be controlling. You generally attract a submissive partner. If you have a *submissive* energetic pattern you tend to allow others to make decisions for you. You generally attract a dominant partner.

If you have a *passive-aggressive* energetic pattern, you may appear to submit to others, but you will fight back secretly. You generally attract a dominant partner or a passive-aggressive one like you. If you have *evasive/withdrawing* pattern, you will avoid commitment and intimacy. You generally attract a partner who is unavailable.

You may find it helpful to compare your energetic stance to that of each of your parents. Often you will emulate one parent and attract someone who is like the other parent.

It is important for you to understand your energetic stance and to know the type of person you are attracting into your energy field. The only way you can attract a different type of partner is to shift your energetic pattern.

People Pleasing Patterns

Some people have a pattern of trying to please parents and other authority figures in their lives. They constantly seek approval and validation from others. They try to live the way others want them to live. This prevents them from growing up, individuating, living their own lives and making their own choices.

Even after they leave home, they continue this pattern by seeking approval from and giving their power away to their spouse/partner. Their relationships become codependent. They give up their power, and the partner is happy to take charge and make decisions for them.

You cannot have an equal relationship with someone you are caretaking or who is caretaking you. There is an inherent inequality there. One person is taking too much responsibility and the other person is not taking enough responsibility.

When you take power from someone else and agree to protect and make decisions for him/her, you are entering into a parental relationship with that person. You become the parent, and s/he becomes the child. Such contracts recreate and re-circulate your family of origin wounds.

The following actions will help you to disengage these unhealthy patterns.

• Stop trying to please others or win their approval.

• Set limits with parents and the other authority figures that try to control you, rescue you, or run your life.

• Stand up for yourself and dissociate from people who criticize you or treat you disrespectfully, unfairly or unkindly.

• Stop being a parental figure who tries to influence, control, rescue, criticize, or fix others.

• Understand that you give your power away when you decide for others. You take a false responsibility that does not belong to you. That often prevents you from taking appropriate responsibility for your life.

• Make your own choices and be responsible for them. Allow others to do the same.

• Learn to set healthy limits and boundaries with others.

• Learn to accept the limits and boundaries that others set with you.

• Make the best choice you can and take responsibility for it.

• Be compassionate with yourself. Acknowledge your mistakes and learn from them.

• Understand that no choice is perfect and all choices carry a lesson to be learned.

These are not things that you are going to accomplish overnight, but they are essential for you to begin doing so that you stop giving your power away or appropriating the power of others. The patterns of inequality — dominant/submissive, victim/victimizer, master/slave, masochist/sadist — are mutually abusive and prevent all of us from stepping into our true power and purpose here.

Archetypes of Self-betrayal

Your core wound, core belief and reactive behavior pattern lead to the creation of a False Self designed to help you deal with the pain of your wound, find safety and/or get the love and approval you want. This False Self represents the way you betray yourself in order to get your needs met.

Your specific pattern of self-betrayal often crystallizes into an archetype or sub-personality. For example, suppose your wound is *abandonment* because Mommy was very ill when you were young and she was unable to take care of you. You manifested the archetype of the *Caretaker* because you developed the core belief *my needs do not matter* and the reactive behavior pattern of *staying and shutting down emotionally*. As the *Caretaker* you believe that you can find love and acceptance only if you deny your own needs and take care of the needs of others. So that becomes your MO in life, not just with Mommy, but in all close relationships.

On the other hand, suppose Mommy ignores you because she has a demanding job and five other children to care for. You have to find some way to get Mommy's attention, so you become the *Bad Boy* or the *Bully*. You develop the core belief

If I don't make trouble I won't be seen, and your reactive pattern is *stay and fight.* The *Bad Boy archetype* works for you because whenever you beat up one of your siblings or get in trouble at school you finally get Mommy's attention. Since negative attention is better than no attention, you learn to accept Mommy's anger as the price you have to pay for love.

The Defender, the Victim, and the Escape Artist

Each of the three reactive behavior patterns — fight, flight, stay and shut down emotionally — has archetypes associated with it. Here are a few to think about:

- **Defender archetypes** are an attempt to protect the child. They are connected with the *stay and fight* reactive behavior pattern. Examples include the *Bully,* the *Bitch,* the *Bad Boy/Girl,* the *General or Drill Sergeant,* the *Amazon Warrior,* and the *Judge/Critic.* Defenders usually exhibit dominant, controlling behavior. They externalize their anger.

- **Victim archetypes** are an attempt to shoulder adult responsibilities at an early age in order to gain the acceptance and love of parents or siblings. They are connected with the *Stay and Shut Down Reactive Behavior Pattern.* Examples include the *Caretaker,* the *Workaholic,* the *Nurse,* the *Martyr,* the *Slave,* the *Whore,* the *Good Boy/Girl and* the *Clown.* Victims usually exhibit submissive or passive-aggressive behavior. They internalize their anger.

- **Escapist archetypes** are an attempt to avoid conflict and responsibility. They are connected with the *withdrawal/flight* reactive behavior pattern. Examples include the *Wild*

Horsie, the *Wild Child,* the *Hare,* the *Artist,* the *Hermit,* the *Magical Child,* the *Don Juan* and the *Femme Fatale.* Escapists usually exhibit isolating, disconnecting, avoiding behavior. They tend to internalize their anger until it is triggered and they leave.

These archetypes are explored in greater depth in Phase Two of the *Real Happiness Workshop Curriculum.* For more information, please refer to both the *Participant's Guide* and the *Facilitator's Manual.*

Over-protected/Under-protected Children

There are two primary reasons that a child does not grow up to be a full-fledged adult. One is that the parents are over-protective and the child is controlled and overpowered. The other is that the parents are under-protective and the child is given too much freedom and too little support.

The over-protected child is given too many limits and never becomes confident, skillful or independent. The parent gives the child the subtle or not-so-subtle message: "You can't do it." The child is rewarded for staying small and weak. Later in life, s/he will have great difficulty taking responsibility for herself. S/he may have trouble keeping a job, going to school, or raising a family.

For example the *Good Girl/Boy* does what Mommy/Daddy wants him or her to do. Clear limits are set for the child. The wounding in this case happens because those limits are not relaxed as the child grows up, and the child often has a difficult time breaking away from the parental control and becoming self-sufficient.

On the other hand, the under-protected child can also have a difficult time keeping a job, going to school, or raising a family. S/he goes out into the world with a false confidence, without sufficient skill or preparation, and inevitably fails. It isn't her fault, but she cannot help concluding, "There must be something wrong with me . . . I can't do it."

For example, the *Bad Boy/Girl* fights any kind of control or domination. S/he learns to scream, hit, throw temper tantrums, or run away. S/he has discipline problems and is often an embarrassment to the parents. Although defiant toward authority figures, s/he does not have real self-confidence, but rather a kind of bravado/overconfidence that results from being allowed to act out without limits or consequences.

Like the *Bad Boy/Girl,* the *Wild Child* is under-protected. S/he is neglected, abandoned or ignored by parents and doesn't receive any limits, rules, or supervision. S/he is left to supervise herself because the parents don't show up to do the job. The parents are insecure and lack confidence. They do not assert their authority as parents or set limits for the child. The child is allowed to do what s/he wants to do. Given this adult-like freedom, without discipline, limits, or expectations from the parents, the *Wild Child* becomes selfish, entitled, and unsocial.

Both under-protected and overprotected children can be severely wounded. Usually, in an attempt to avoid the type of parenting they grew up with, they adopt the opposite parenting pattern with their own children. Overprotected children give their kids too much freedom. Under-protected children are often controlling of their kids.

What was your experience as a child? What is your parenting style with your children?

The Sub-personalities of the False Self

All of the sub-personalities that comprise the False Self are wound-driven and created in shame and in fear. These sub-personalities lock you into limiting roles that arbitrarily separate you from others or saddle you with inappropriate responsibilities that burden you and prevent you from growing and stepping into your power.

All sub-personalities are psychological/energetic structures that cause you to abandon and betray your Core Self. They all lead to dysfunctional, codependent relationships that keep the cycle of abuse in place.

As long as you are living out these archetypes of self-betrayal you will be showing up as a victim or a victimizer. You will be someone who plays a dominant role, a submissive role, a passive-aggressive role or an evasive role. While all of these roles are adopted as survival strategies, they ultimately do not satisfy you. In the end, you will come to realize that self-betrayal is too high a price to pay for survival.

Until you have that recognition, your False Self remains in place, along with all of its archetypes of self-betrayal. But one day the psychological pain of self-betrayal escalates. You grow weary of attempting to show up as other people want or expect you to. You quit the job and/or leave the relationship in which you abdicate your power or attempt to control others. You refuse to take another step forward as a victim or a victimizer.

Some people make a conscious choice to shift their lives out of self-betrayal, while others need a little help from the universe. When we can't take the bull by the horns, the bull may take us on, and it may not be pretty. Jobs and marriages can end suddenly. Unexpected health issues can arise. Accidents can happen. Something generally occurs that gets our attention and tells us unmistakably that the status quo must change.

Taking Your Power Back

In order to take your power back you must first see how you give it away. Do you trade your freedom for security? Do you let others make decisions for you because you lack confidence or fear failure? Do you find that you frequently play a submissive role in close relationships? Do you hate change and avoid taking risks? In what ways do you hold yourself back or depend on others?

Conversely, are you a caretaker who likes to take on responsibility and enjoys making decisions for others? Do you get inappropriately involved in other people's lives? Are you intrusive or controlling? Do you cross boundaries and ignore limits that others have tried to set? Do you impose your ideas and values on others? Do you frequently play a dominating role in your close relationships?

Or are you an escape artist who refuses to control or be controlled? Are you so sensitive to the words and actions of others that at the first sign of struggle or discord you are off to the races? Do you fear intimacy with others? Do you have trouble making commitments? When a relationship or a job ends, are you the one to leave?

What are the behavior patterns that keep repeating in your life? What do you fear? What do you try to avoid? What pushes your buttons and sets your reactive behavior pattern in motion?

It is not easy to look at all this, but it is essential if you want to stop giving your power away and start learning to trust yourself and others. We all give our power away and/or misappropriate the power of others. We all have trust issues. You don't need to be ashamed about this. You just need to see your pattern so that you can begin to make different choices.

For example, if you are showing up as the *Martyr* or the *Caretaker* in all of your relationships your emotional needs will not be met. Your belief *my needs don't matter* is running your life.

People who are looking for caretakers are spontaneously attracted to you. And if you meet someone who doesn't need a caretaker, there is no attraction on your part. Your belief *I won't get love if I don't take care of you compels you* into the same type of role over and over again.

You can change this only if you become aware of it and begin to consciously say "No" when needy people come into your life. When the person with crutches approaches you and asks for a place to stay, you override your desire to invite him home and nurse him back to health. You tell him, "I see you are attracted to me because I have been a good caretaker in the past, but I am done with that role. Now I am learning how to take care of myself."

As you learn to stand up for yourself and reject the old dysfunctional roles you played in order to get love from others, you find that you are able to bring love and acceptance directly to yourself. You care for yourself. You become your own nurse. And you begin to heal the wound behind the false belief *my needs don't matter.* As the wound heals, the belief falls away, and so does the role that results from it.

Now when someone asks, "Will all the caretakers please stand up?" you learn to hunker down in your chair. The muscles in your legs may tighten because they are used to answering the call, but they will learn in time to relax. You have shifted from the inside out. You no longer have the same MO.

As your self-betrayal and the patterns that support it come to an end, you are free to be yourself. That is the moment of true liberation. At that moment your healing journey is substantially complete and you can begin to step into your true power and purpose.

Important Questions to Ask Yourself

> What is my reactive behavior pattern: fight/flight or stay and shut down emotionally?

> Am I dominant and controlling, passive and submissive, or evasive and afraid of intimacy/commitment?

> Did I learn this from one or both of my parents?

> Do I have a pattern of making decisions for others or allowing others to make decisions for me?

> In what ways do I need to make my own decisions and tell others to back off and allow me to choose for myself?

> In what ways do I need to back off and give others the space to make their own decisions?

> What limits do I need to set with others in order to take my power back?

> What limits do I need to respect in order to stop taking power from others?

> What sub-personalities did I develop to survive as a child and in what way have they reinforced my self-betrayal?

> What roles do I need to reject in order to stop betraying myself and begin stepping into my power and purpose?

Surrender the False Self

GOAL

Give up limiting roles and beliefs.

STRATEGY

Drop your story.

As I said before, you aren't going to change your belief by saying a bunch of affirmations that you don't really believe at a gut level. To change your belief, you have to love yourself radically and realize that you bought into an untrue story about who you are.

Your archetype of self-betrayal — the sub-personality you adopted to get your needs met in life — is the essence of your story. You chose to be the *Martyr* or the *Bad Boy* or the *Perpetual Child* because when you showed up in that role you got acceptance and love. But that role was just a role. It was not who you are.

Understand that you felt unsafe and unsupported in being who you are. That is why you chose to be someone else. You were smart enough to see what others wanted or expected of you and you tried your best to become that. Perhaps you succeeded. Maybe you had a good mask and played your role convincingly. Or maybe your mask wasn't that good, nor was your performance. You know to what extent you bought and sold the story about you.

If are good at acting out the story you might believe that the role you play is who are. You might believe in your own lies and pretensions. If so, it will be harder for you to see how the story sells you short. As long as you and those around you believe the story, you aren't going to feel the pain and self-betrayal around it.

But sooner or later, the story about you is going to self-destruct, because it is untrue. It can't be sustained forever. The mask begins to crack. The role begins to be uncomfortable. The self-betrayal becomes palpable and the story is questioned, perhaps for the first time. You ask, "Is this who I really am?" or "Is this who I really want to be?" And the answer is "No!"

If you are wise, you realize that Humpty Dumpty is about to come off the wall and you get some therapy or join a support group. It's hard to watch the story crash into hundreds of pieces when those pieces at one time seemed to belong to you. Often, it's even harder for your husband or wife to watch your life fall apart, because they probably still believe the story you told them about you. Even your friends, your kids, your coworkers and fellow church members still believe that story.

The revolutionary fact is that while they may all believe it, you don't believe it anymore. Don't make the mistake of trying to turn to any of them for support and understanding. They are invested in the "old you." The "new you" is unpredictable, maybe even terrifying. They might even suspect that you are a bit daffy and try to get you to check into a loony bin.

Don't blame them. They really can't help it. They want the "old you" back and they don't realize yet that the person they used to know — the one who played her role so impeccably — is gone forever.

Find a healing community that will support your transformation. Find people who will support you in becoming authentic and telling the truth about who you are. Take some time off from your old roles and responsibilities. You have a hard time showing up for them anyway. You may even find it impossible to continue with them. Your heart just isn't in them anymore.

So take a break. Make time for your mid-life crisis. Your values are shifting. It is not possible for you to betray yourself or give your power away anymore. It is not possible for you to put on your mask and go to work or put on your smiley face and cook dinner. Those days are over.

Understand the signs of crisis and give yourself time and space to go though it. Otherwise, you will experience excruciating pain. When it is time for the shift to come, you need to cooperate with it. Life is a much better mid-wife when you create a gentle supportive space for the baby (your True Self) to be born.

You need to understand that this is serious business. Your life is on the line here, so don't blow it off. Don't ignore the warning signs. When Shiva rises up to smite your life and bring you to your knees, please cooperate. Don't try to hold onto your old life anymore. Surrender. Get on you knees. Let the old roles be taken from you so that they are no longer a burden to you.

You are like a caterpillar going into the transformational sac. Once you enter the birthing chamber, the old you is gone. You can't turn around and come back out. Those sixteen legs that used to carry you across the ground have been absorbed into the amniotic fluid. They don't exist anymore. There is no way to resist the process. You must go through it. So please relax. Let the False Self die and the True Self be born.

When you emerge you will have brightly colored wings. You will no longer have to labor tediously on the ground. You will spread your wings and fly. All the masks will be gone. The roles will vanish. The archetypes of self-betrayal will be transmuted into archetypes of transformation and empowerment.

The truth is that the time of the second birth — the spiritual transformation — comes for everyone. Not all decide to heed the call. Some stay in self-betrayal and never grow their spiritual wings. They are difficult learners. They don't know how to trust themselves or anyone else. They will be reborn as caterpillars and take the journey a second or a third time. That's okay. Patience is a virtue. We all have to learn it.

But those who know that the story is a lie must drop the story. It has served its purpose. It is no longer needed. Like an old skin, it needs to be dropped. The new skin is grown organically as the old one is cast away. The new story with its new empowering beliefs cannot be written until the old one is disproved and discarded.

Birth and death go hand in hand. Like the Phoenix, the True Self is born out of the ashes of the False Self. The dazzling light of love incarnate is experienced at the end of the Dark Night of the Soul. Out of pain comes wisdom and understanding. Out of self-betrayal comes the True Self who can never be betrayed. S/he lives in all of us. And when all that is false has been rejected, s/he is spontaneously born.

Each one of us is a shining being with great love to give and a great purpose to serve. The True Self knows how to give and receive that love and fulfill that purpose. That is why her birth into the world is of paramount importance.

The Christ Self, Buddha Nature, Essential Tao

It does not matter if you are inspired by Moses, or Christ, or Krishna, or Buddha, or Lao Tzu. All of the great wisdom traditions talk about the birth of the True Self. What is important is that you realize that the True Self is not about somebody else. It is about you.

You are the bringer of love. You are the anointed one. You are the one who arises as the light in the darkness. You are the voice in the wilderness. Unless you come into the fullness of your power and purpose, redemption does not come to the world. Jesus came to show us that. So did Buddha. So did all the masters.

Your awakening, healing and empowerment is of paramount importance. Please do not think that you come here without gifts to give or the power to give them. Like all human beings, you are here to be an instrument of love and forgiveness. If you need another purpose than this then you do not understand the great journey you are taking. You don't understand why you have suffered and learned from your mistakes, why you have fallen down and risen up. You don't understand that you are here not just to awaken and heal, but also to lead and to serve.

The earth grows dim without the light of the sun upon it. The Spirit is hidden away and forgotten without the presence of the light-bearers. They have come as you have to light the way for God's people. But they could not play this role had they not discovered the light within themselves.

Once you discover the light within, you carry it forth into the world. That is why you are here.

The Good News

The good news is that you are not here to be a caterpillar crawling on the ground. You are here to be transformed into a brightly colored butterfly drinking the nectar of the most beautiful flowers. That is not just true for you. It is true for everyone.

Please do not underestimate the power or the purpose of the journey. Understand that when the time for transformation comes it must be honored. Step Eight tells you to drop the past so that the old can die and the new can be born in your life.

Sometimes it is scary to let go of what is familiar. But holding onto it does not work anymore. If you try, things become more difficult. So you learn to let go, because letting go advances the transformational process.

Let the old definitions of self fade way. You must come to know yourself all over again. You are like a newborn babe. You don't know who you are yet. You must take the time to find out who you are and what you care about. This time, you are your own parent and guide. No one else is going to be looking over your shoulder or telling you what to believe or what to do. You are both the witness and the participant, the one who speaks and the one who listens.

Jesus said, "I am the way, the truth and the life." The same is now true for you. The way has been cleared before you. The truth about you is revealed. And your life is unfolding. Your job is simply to honor what is true, what feels right, what happens spontaneously and without struggle. You are here to let the Great Way — the Tao — unfold through you.

Tao moves confidently like a river flowing to the sea. It circles around branches and boulders, accommodating and dancing with all of the obstacles, until they cease to be obstacles and re-join with the flow of the river.

When the True Self is born, the personal life and the impersonal one join as one. Now you are fully yourself, individuated and unique, and you are also ready to play your part in the collective journey. Until you individuated and dropped your story, you could not play a role in the healing of human consciousness on planet earth. You might have tried, but until self-betrayal falls away all attempts to serve others inevitably fail. One who is wound-driven cannot help others heal their wounds. But now that self-betrayal has come to an end your purpose as a healer and a light-bearer can be revealed.

You do not need to figure any of this out. Step Eight tells you just to drop your story. The new story will unfold by itself. It cannot and will not be imposed from the outside. It will evolve in its own leisurely time from the inside out. When you are ready, the call will come, and you will answer it, even if you don't know how.

All that you used to do for yourself and by yourself will now be done in a different way. Spirit will make its Will known within your heart and your hands and feet will move with its bidding. The words that you need to speak will be upon your lips when they need to be spoken. And actions of Spirit will flow through you as the water flows in the river bed, playfully and with confidence. For the True Self is in charge, and the False Self has fallen away.

Important Questions to Ask Yourself

> What false beliefs about myself, if any, am I still holding onto?

> In what way am I still clinging to my past, with all its pain, lack of authenticity, and repeated self-betrayal?

> What is the payoff for holding onto the past?

> What is the core belief I want to question and shift?

> What roles or archetypes of self-betrayal result from this belief?

> What is my story in a nutshell and in what ways is it untrue?

> When did I realize that my story was untrue and was holding me back from living a fulfilling life?

> Can I drop this story and be naked and unfettered?

> Am I going through a transformational death/rebirth process right now in my life?

> Am I surrendering to it or resisting it?

> Can I let go and trust the process?

> Can I let my False Self die and my True Self be born?

Weathering Spiritual Crisis

This is a time when there is a major paradigm shift in our lives. It is a time when the old patterns driven by fear and shame must end, and the new spirit and love-directed patterns must begin.

This does not happen overnight, nor does it happen in a neat or pretty way. Sometimes old patterns die hard. Sometimes new patterns are very slow to emerge. It can feel awkward and look messy.

For many of us, some kind of spiritual crisis accompanies the paradigm shift. The old is dying and the new is not yet born, so there can be a sense of disorientation and even hopelessness here. Old values and beliefs, friendships, family and social structures no longer support us. We are in a kind of strange limbo.

Our spiritual practice of connecting to love helps us to prepare for the transformation we all have to make from the caterpillar stage to the butterfly stage of our lives. It enables us to trust the process of emotional healing and psychological growth that prepares us to make the quantum leap from a fear-driven life to a love-directed life.

In order to grow, we all go into a chrysalis state. We stop moving outward and begin to move inward. We stop looking for love and acceptance outside and begin to seek it within. This is the turning point in our lives.

In the chrysalis state, we learn to bring love and acceptance to our own experience. That sends a message to our soul that we are ready to consciously participate in the process of our spiritual birth. When we consciously participate in this process, it does not have to be sudden, painful or disorienting.

We cannot easily go through this spiritual rebirth experience without wrapping ourselves in the love of our Core Self and feeling the love of the Great Mother, whose only prayer is that we give birth to all that is true within us. If we don't cultivate the practice of bringing love to ourselves, we will be too scared to let go of the False Self. It will seem like we are letting go into an abyss.

This is a time when we need a lot of support. We need our true friends and members of our spiritual family or community to hold the space for us. We often need the help of a skilled therapist, guide or mentor who has made this journey and knows how to help us find our bearings.

This time of transformation is often referred to in spiritual writings as the *Dark Night of the Soul.* It is dark because all that we used to depend on is stripped away from us. It is an intense crisis in which we have to find a new faith and a new meaning for our lives. Often, this happens as a kind of mid-age crisis when it is time for old roles and responsibilities to be questioned. Occasionally, it happens to people at a younger age.

Of course, not everyone engages in emotional healing and spiritual practices to connect to the Core Self. Not everyone moves organically into a state of letting go of the old and unburdening. Not everyone has the support of a spiritual community or spiritual therapist. Some people call for change at a soul level, but they do not understand what they are asking for. They want their lives to get better but they do not know that for change to come the structure of denial must crumble.

They resist growth and stay in jobs, relationships, and other roles/structures long beyond the point where they have outgrown them. In order to awaken, their soul creates some kind of a storm or healing crisis in their lives. Perhaps they get sick or have an accident. Someone close to them might die or they might have a near death experience. Their house might burn down; their marriage might fall apart; they might be fired or laid off from a job they have been doing for twenty years. They might check themselves into a drug/alcohol treatment facility. In one way or another, they hit bottom. They know that they have to change. There is simply no turning back.

Yet, for those of us who heed the warning signs, the death/ rebirth process does not need to be sudden or dramatic. We can see our patterns of self-betrayal and begin to shift them.

We can release ourselves from our boxes and prisons before they become unbearable. We can take Humpty Dumpty down from the wall before the ground begins to tremble. We can do this consciously and progressively because we have made the connection to our Core Self and we are ready to live out the creative blueprint we were born with.

Before we take our leap of faith, we know there is land on the other side of the chasm. We know we are moving out of roles and responsibilities that we have outgrown. We are consciously shedding our old skin. We are laying down our burdens and beginning to open to a new vision of our life.

PART THREE

~

Empowerment

Real Happiness Roadmap

PHASE THREE

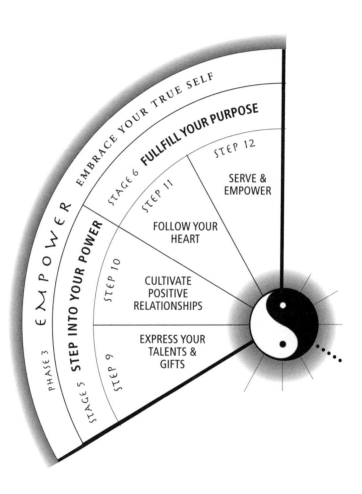

PHASE 3 · EMPOWER · EMBRACE YOUR TRUE SELF

STAGE 5 · STEP INTO YOUR POWER

STAGE 6 · FULLFILL YOUR PURPOSE

STEP 9 · EXPRESS YOUR TALENTS & GIFTS

STEP 10 · CULTIVATE POSITIVE RELATIONSHIPS

STEP 11 · FOLLOW YOUR HEART

STEP 12 · SERVE & EMPOWER

STEP

9

~

Express Your Talents & Gifts

GOAL

Do what you love to do.

STRATEGY

Be creative. Take risks.

Now that you have progressed into the empowerment phase of the work, it is time to stop doing what you don't want to do and begin to do what you want to do. Self-betrayal must end. Self-honoring must begin.

Forcing yourself to do work that does not honor you or engage your creative passion leads to depression. There will be no energy or joy in your life. There needs to be a relinquishment of this pattern.

See how in the past you lived the life that others wanted you to live. In the process, you abandoned some of your key interests, passions and gifts. Now it is time for you to follow your heart and embrace your gifts.

Get in touch with what you really want and are willing to show up for. If you do not care about the work you do, if you are not truly committed to it, you will continue to live in self-betrayal. Don't do that anymore. Give yourself the time and space to live your dreams.

Your creative energy comes back when you honor yourself and do what you love to do. That is what makes you joyful, and then your energy can express with natural enthusiasm and touch the hearts of others.

If you have an unhealed father wound, you may need to develop your self confidence by taking little steps toward reaching your goals. Small successes lead to greater ones.

Shooting too high or moving too fast will result in self-destruction and reinforce past failures along with the shame associated with them.

Honoring Yourself on All Levels

There are four components that must be present if you are to fulfill your life purpose:

1. Spiritual: express your gift and serve others (purpose)

2. Mental: see and know what you want to achieve (vision)

3. Emotional: have a strong desire to achieve it (passion)

4. Physical: show up, be grounded, have a practical strategy (commitment)

First you need to know what your gift is. Don't be surprised if you don't have a clue. Most of us abandon our gifts at an early age in order to get the approval of Mommy or Daddy. They want us to make them proud. They want us to walk in their footsteps. They may want us to fulfill their unfulfilled desires and achieve the goals they were unable to achieve. They have their own agenda for our lives. So do our teachers and mentors.

Few people encourage us to be ourselves and to find out what we naturally enjoy and excel at doing. As a result, the creative blueprint for our embodiment that abides in our Core Self may go unrecognized. We probably spend the first thirty years of our lives trying to show up as Mommy, Daddy, teachers, ministers and other mentors wanted us to. We took our marching orders and began to march toward the approval they dangled before our eyes.

The problem is that this was a march of self-betrayal. We attended law school and became an attorney because that is what Daddy wanted us to be. We married a doctor or a dentist because that is what Mommy wanted for us. They wanted us to have security. They wanted to make sure that we were safe and that the bills would be paid. Perhaps they also wanted us to have some of the other socially desired symbols of success: an expensive car, a beautiful home, well behaved children, and a good reputation in church and community.

We followed their roadmap for our lives. We thought it was the one we were supposed to have. But we never verified that. Turns out it was a rather expensive assumption. Thirty of forty years later, we might wake up and ask, "What the hell am I doing?" That, I suppose, is part of the learning process. First you betray yourself so that you know what not to do. And then you learn from your mistake and begin to honor who you are.

That's what our mid-life crisis gives us the opportunity to do. We reassess and reinvent our lives. No matter how much self-betrayal exists in our past, it's never too late to discover our inner blueprint and begin to honor it. The tragedy is not that we come to truth late. The tragedy would be that we never come to it at all.

Mental/Emotional Blocks

Having abandoned our blueprint, we need a strategy for rediscovering it. The first place we need to look is within our own consciousness. We have been taking our direction from the outside far too long. Now it is time to look within.

There are two primary actions you need to take:

- Stop doing what you do not want to do.

- Ask yourself what you want to do and begin doing it.

This doesn't seem like such a hard formula to implement, yet people have huge resistance to both of these steps. They think they can do what they hate and what they love to do at the same time. That seems like it is less of a risk. The problem is that after they finish doing what they hate to do they have no energy left over to do what they love.

They live in a double bind world, a world of continual Catch 22s. Their motto is "I want to, but I can't." The truth is that they "can" but they don't really want to. They do not desire change enough. They do not hate their self-betrayal sufficiently to abandon it. They try to grab the new while holding onto the old. But the truth is they can't really grab onto anything new if they are holding onto the past. It doesn't work.

Letting go of the past is absolutely essential if we want to move into our power and purpose. So we need to see our resistance honestly and clearly. We don't have to beat ourselves up. We just have to realize "I have a lot of resistance here. I am not ready to take a big step . . . maybe there is a small step I can take."

And so instead of quitting our job, we cut back on our hours and give ourselves one day or two mornings a week to explore what we love. That is both honest and realistic. It acknowledges our resistance without allowing it to undermine our progress forward.

The key here is to move out of the Catch 22 scenario and end the untrue, self-sabotaging belief "I want to, but I can't." As I have said many times before to my clients and students, "Stop telling me what you *can't do* and tell me what you *can do.*" What you can't do is none of my business. And it really should not be yours either. It is not an empowering idea. It is the language of a victim. Remember, in Phase Three, there are no victims, so don't be one. In Phase Three there are only creators. Be the creator of your life.

You don't have to be flashy and take big, sweeping steps. Small steps are fine. In some way, they are preferable to big steps because they lay the groundwork for the big steps. They create the foundation that you will build on when you are ready.

Connecting with Your Desire

Many people say, "I want to do this or that," but they are just kidding themselves and everyone else. I can't tell you how many people have told me, "I want to write a book." I always tell them "Great idea!" But then when I run into them in six months or a year I ask them, "How's the book coming?" and they look at me like I am from some other planet. "What book is that?" they ask. "The one you told be you were going to write six months ago," I remind them.

"Oh," they say and then proceed to tell me all of the reasons why they couldn't write it. "Save your breath," I want to say. "You might need it for something you really want to do."

The bottom line is that you will only do what you really want to do. Writing a book isn't what you want to do or you would do it. Nobody has to tell a writer when or how to write, or an artist when or how to paint. Nobody has to motivate a musician to practice or a swimmer to swim laps. All of these people are doing what they want to do. The motivation comes from within.

Of course when you spend the first thirty years of life doing what other people want you to do, you might have a little difficulty getting in touch with what you want to do. You haven't had much practice tuning into your desires. This is a skill that you have to learn.

So be honest about it. Don't try to impress your friend who runs marathons by telling him you are training for a 5K when you haven't had a day's exercise in the last twenty years. Don't tell people what they want to hear. Tell them the truth. Tell them, "I have no idea what I want to do. I have spent my whole life listening to others. I'm a novice here."

You can't start your journey to empowerment by lying to yourself or others. You have to be honest. And you have to take the time to get emotionally connected to yourself. You have to keep asking the question "What do I want?" or "What feels good to me?" until the answer comes.

Please don't be impatient or put pressure on yourself. That just slows down the process. Take the time and the space that you need to connect with your true desire. Only when you know what you really want and care about will you be ready to move forward. Until then, just "Do no harm." Refrain from self-betrayal.

It is a simple truth that caring and commitment go hand in hand. You can commit to the desire of your heart. You can show up for it every day. You can do what needs to be done. You can overcome obstacles. You can get up when you fall down because you are moving toward a goal you really care about.

You can't do that when you don't care about something. All you can do is show up like a zombie and go through the motions. A lot of people live their lives like that. But not you. For you those days are over.

Healing with Daddy

Father wounds hold us back from doing what we love to do. We don't have the self-confidence, the belief in ourselves, and the needed preparation to succeed. We don't know what our gifts are or, if we do, we don't trust them. We don't know how to show up and get things done.

When you haven't had the father energy modeled for you, you often have difficulty taking risks, or you take foolish ones. You need to learn to take small steps toward your goals. You have to stay grounded and put one foot in front of the other.

People with daddy wounds often dismiss the preparation phase and try to skip steps. As a result they keep falling down. Yet they don't learn from their mistakes. They keep shooting for the stars, crashing to the ground and burning. They are often addicted to speed. They do things fast, but not necessarily well. They include the *Hare* and the *Speed Demon* sub-personalities. Their incessant activity is driven by fear and insecurity. They are impatient and under-prepared.

Others who show up in bad form are the *Charlatan* who knows how to fake it but can't make it, the *Scam Artist,* who knows how to sell it but can't deliver it, the *Bullshit Artist* who talks big but can't walk his talk, and the *Leap Frog,* who skips over the necessary steps.

On the other hand, some people who have father wounds can't get out the door. They are just as wounded. They do not trust or express their gifts because they are afraid of rejection. They stay in their shell and hide. Often they over-prepare and obsess on details. They make everything much harder and more complicated than it is. Their belief is "I am not ready to do it." They include the *Procrastinator,* the *Dreamer,* the *Professional Student,* and the *Perfectionist.* They insist on taking time to get more skills and training. That's true even if they have already earned six PhDs. They are under-motivated and over-prepared.

On the other hand, the *Workaholic,* the *Martyr,* the *Slave,* and the *Savior* or *Guru* believe "I have to do it. If I didn't do it no one else would." They think that they are here to sacrifice their own needs in order to meet the needs of others. They are here to fulfill their duty, to serve, save, or redeem others. They aren't here to enjoy their work or to have fun doing it.

If you have manifested any of these sub-personalities, you have ignored your true talents and gifts and given your power away. You have spent your life preparing for something you don't want to do, doing something you hate, or sacrificing your joy and fulfillment in order to please or meet the expectations of others.

All this happened because Daddy was unable to show up for you or showed up in an unhealthy way. He was either absent from your life, physically and/or emotionally, or he was always breathing down your neck telling you what to do and how to do it. If Daddy was the critic, chances are you internalized his opinion of you. Chances are you feel inferior, just as Daddy did. Chances are he passed his wound onto you.

Often you have to take some time to heal with Daddy in order to move into your power and learn to express your talents and gifts. Don't be surprised if an opportunity to stand up to Daddy or to make peace with him comes into your life when you are working on this step. It happens for many people.

Natural Gifts and Experiential Gifts

Natural talents/gifts are the gifts at birth that you came into this life to nurture, develop and ultimately express. These may be creative gifts, emotional gifts, intellectual gifts or physical gifts.

We all know people who are talented singers, dancers, painters, writers, or entertainers. They uplift others by sharing their creative gifts. We also know great teachers, lawyers, doctors or business people who excel using their intellects. We have met therapists, nurses, and a variety of caregivers who support and heal others with their emotional gifts. And we know great athletes who amaze and entertain us with their physical gifts.

You may have more than one of these gifts. You may also have paranormal gifts like clairvoyance or clairaudience, or spiritual gifts like inner wisdom or connection to healing energies.

If you are lucky, you were able to tune into your gifts at an early age and begin to actively nurture them with the support of your parents. If you are not so lucky, your parents may have ignored your gifts or pushed you in a different direction. Or perhaps your parents put a lot of pressure on you to develop your gifts, and you developed a bad taste and turned away from using your talents.

Hopefully, you have begun to heal whatever wounds you received here and can return to reclaim your gifts on your own terms. This will make it easier for you to value your gifts, heal any money issues you have and connect with the natural flow of abundance in your life.

In addition to the gifts that you were born with, you also have experiential gifts and talents that you have learned in this lifetime by facing challenges and hardships. By learning your lessons and healing your wounds, you bring new skills to the table that can help you express your natural gifts. Indeed, it is the combination of your natural and experiential gifts that enables you to show up where you are needed in life and fulfill your true creative purpose.

Step Nine asks you to make a conscious effort to do what you love to do and be open to opportunities to share your gifts whenever they present themselves. If you have not nurtured your gifts, begin to develop them through study, training, apprenticeship, or volunteer activities so that you can acquire the skills and experience needed for success. Be sure to set realistic, obtainable goals and learn to take small steps toward reaching them.

Be patient and committed. Learn to show up even when it's hard. And let go of your perfectionism. It is a major obstacle to self-expression.

Be willing to take risks and push through resistance. You can't stay locked within your comfort zone or you will not grow and step into your power. Say yes to new opportunities. Walk through the open doors. Don't let fear or habitual paralysis hold you back. See obstacles as challenges instead of setbacks. Accept the outcome and learn from your mistakes. Don't give up. Believe in yourself and keep moving forward.

Important Questions to Ask Yourself

> Do I know what my gifts are? If so what are they?

> What do I desire? What is joyful for me? What do I care about? What can I commit to showing up for?

> Was I encouraged to develop and express my gifts by my parents, siblings and teachers?

> Was I pushed in a different direction by parents/teachers/siblings or did they put pressure on me to perform?

> What father wounds do I have that make it difficult for me to find fulfillment in my work and career?

> Do I have a pattern of setting unrealistic goals, shooting too high, and failing?

> Do I have a pattern of procrastinating, making excuses, not taking risks?

> How is this related to my father wound?

> Do I have an opportunity right now to heal some aspect of my father wound?

> Do I have money issues? Do I have difficulty valuing my gifts?

> What are my experiential gifts and how have I integrated them with my natural gifts?

> What is my greatest failure in life? What have I learned from this?

> What is my greatest achievement in life?

> Do I have the skills necessary to express my passion and my vision? If not, how will I acquire them?

> How can my gifts can be used to serve others with wounds/ beliefs similar to my own?

> What would I like my career to look like five years from now?

> What steps can I take right now to trust my gifts and to move into my power and purpose?

10

~

Cultivate Positive, Equal Relationships With Others

GOAL

Experience equality and intimacy with others.

STRATEGY

Own your triggers. Practice forgiveness.

In an empowered relationship people are equals. Each person pulls her own weight and takes responsibility for loving and supporting herself. No one is saving the other, fixing the other, deciding for or controlling the other. When you move into Phase Three of this transformational process you are leaving behind codependent relationships in which both people give their power away and cultivating positive relationships based on equality and mutual trust. You are no longer showing up as either a victim or a victimizer. You have substantially ended the chain of abuse and the patterns of self-betrayal in your life.

That means that you are no longer living to please, take care of, or control someone else, nor are you living to be taken care of, controlled or dominated by another person. You are not accepting any one else's authority over you, nor are you claiming to be an authority for anyone else.

You understand and practice good boundaries in your relationships. You know what your responsibility is and isn't and what the other person's responsibility is and isn't. You use my *Crash Course in Boundaries* as a regular practice, taking responsibility for what you think, feel, say and do, and allowing others to take responsibility for their thoughts, feelings, words and actions. (See my book *The Keys to the Kingdom* for this and other important spiritual practices that can keep you and your partnership on track.)

This isn't to say that you do this perfectly. You don't. You make mistakes and so does your partner. But you are both committed to acknowledging your mistakes and learning from them.

That means that you do not need to be right all the time or to constantly make your partner wrong. You know that sometimes you see things more clearly than your partner does and sometimes s/he is more clear than you are. You don't compete to be "better than" the other and you don't accept the idea that you are "less than."

While feelings of inferiority may come up for both of you, you don't buy into them. You see that such feelings are bringing up something in you that needs to be accepted, forgiven and healed. You see that the little girl or boy in you is not feeling loved and you learn to bring love to him or her when s/he needs it.

You understand that your number one responsibility is to love and honor yourself and you do not try to make your partner responsible for loving you and making you happy. You understand that happiness comes from the inside. It comes from developing a loving relationship with yourself, and that is an ongoing process in your life. Each day you are learning to show up for yourself in a more loving and compassionate way.

While you love and cherish your partner, you understand that your partner must take responsibility for loving and honoring himself or herself. You cannot take on that responsibility on without becoming codependent and sabotaging the relationship. So you learn to stand back and give your partner the time and space to work out any issues of self-worth that are arising. You know that it is your partner's responsibility to be the bringer of love to his or her own experience.

In spite of all this, there are times when you trespass on each other. You project your fear and shame. You try to blame the other person. It is always painful when this happens. Moreover, the trust between you can be undermined if you are not successful in forgiving each other and making amends.

Your greatest commitment therefore is and must continue to be to forgive your partner and yourself for your mutual trespasses. To do so you must find a way to listen compassionately to the cries of your little child and your partner's little child. You must feel the pain of the child and work to soothe it and hold the space for healing and acceptance.

Your ability to show up for your partner's little kid is based on your ability to show up for your own. So you learn to take the time your child needs to feel accepted and loved by you, so that your little child will not be jealous of and competitive with your partner's little child.

You understand that two hurt little children cannot love each other. A loving adult is needed. Sometimes that will be you showing up to hold the space of love and acceptance when your partner is triggered. Sometimes it will be your partner holding the space for you. It needs to be a two way street. You must both learn to play the role of peacemaker. Otherwise, the triggers will escalate and neither one of you will feel safe in the relationship.

Two Types of Empowered Relationships

There are two types of empowered relationships. One is "separate but equal" and the other is "shared intimacy."

In the first type of relationship partners need a lot of personal space. Often, they do not live together. Or, if they do, they have clear boundaries that create identifiable personal space for each person.

In the second type of relationship there is a lot of time for sharing and intimacy. People live together, travel together and share most aspects of their lives.

The danger of the first type of relationship is that there will be a lack of intimacy and cohesion. People may feel distant from and unsupported by their partners. The danger of the second type of relationship is that it may become complacent and routine. The partners may take each other for granted and the energy between them may become stale.

The antidote in the first case is time together. The antidote in the second case is time apart.

Some relationships thrive when partners spend a lot of time together and share many interests. Others thrive when each person has plenty of time to do his or her own thing. It is helpful if you know what type of relationship works for you.

In order for intimacy and interest to be sustained, partners must find a balance between time alone and time together. Each person must feel supported in pursuing interests not shared by the other person. On the other hand, consistent time must be devoted to sharing and communicating with each other.

Each couple must work out these dynamics.

Sometimes people are not well matched in terms of the kind of relationship they need. If one person needs a lot of intimacy and the other person is afraid of this and requires a lot of alone time, the needs of both people are not going to be met. For long term success, it is helpful to be with a partner who shares your general idea of how much intimacy or alone time is needed.

People who have individuated early in life may not require a great deal of time away from their partners. They are happy to engage, to create a shared space and a "we" consciousness. This takes them both deeper in their surrender to intimacy and love.

However, when one or both partner(s) needs time to individuate, a "separate but equal" relationship can support them in their personal growth. Such a relationship can be a lifestyle choice, or it can be a step on the way toward greater intimacy with each other or with future partners.

Moving Beyond Romance into a Full-Chakra Union

A successful partnership is grounded and realistic. It does not ask too much or too little from the individuals. Each partner has surrendered the romantic ideal, accepts the other as s/he is and shows up consistently for him or her. Moreover, each person is willing to accept and work through the challenges the relationship brings. There is a solid commitment from both people.

For a partnership to be complete, there must be a sustainable passion in the relationship. Both people must be attracted to each other and desire each other's company. All of the chakras must be engaged. Full-chakra relationships involve connection and a positive exchange of energies in all of the areas listed below.

* Spiritual Connection: You share and/or fully respect/ support each other's unique path of healing and connection to the divine.

* Mental Connection: You share and/or fully respect/ support each other's interests, values and gifts of creative expression. You are able to communicate honestly and respectfully.

* Emotional Connection: You trust each other. You feel accepted, heard and supported by each other. Your hearts are open to each other. You feel grateful for each other and value what you share.

* Physical Connection: You feel attracted to each other and are affectionate in a way that feels good to both of you. You feel safe and secure living together. Your sexual relationship works for both of you.

You might find it helpful to rate your current relationship by assigning a number from one to ten (1-10) to each of the above categories. Give a one for the least degree of connection and a ten for the highest degree of connection. Then add up all the numbers. The highest score your relationship could have would be a 50. The lowest score would be a 5. If you are brave, ask your partner to rate the relationship too and compare notes.

If you both rate your relationship between 40 and 50, then you are fortunate and blessed that you and your partner support each other in your journey to awaken, heal and step into your power and purpose. If you rate your relationship between 30 and 40, then it is still likely that your relationship is an asset and a support for both of you, provided that you are both committed to working together to increase intimacy, communication, and mutual respect.

On the other hand, if you rated your relationship between 20 and 30, then it is probably time for you and your partner to sit down and have a heart-to-heart talk. You need to discover whether you have a common vision and are both fully committed to the relationship. You must each begin to ask the question: "Does the relationship provide a vehicle in which I can honor and express my True Self, or does it limit me from expressing myself authentically?"

This conversation is a necessary one for most couples who have been together for 20 or 30 years. You may have fulfilled your parenting and child-rearing responsibilities together, but that does not necessarily mean that you want to spend another 20 or 30 years together. You and your partner will need to determine if staying together enables both of you to grow and come into your power or if it just reinforces your patterns of self-betrayal.

If you rated your relationship below 20, then it is pretty clear that you don't feel that it supports you in your process of healing and empowerment. You may have to face the possibility that completing your relationship is an important ingredient in relinquishing your patterns of self-betrayal. If this is true for you, it is probably true for you partner too.

Regardless of what you decide, be aware that a relationship cannot be repaired or transformed unless both partners are willing to do things differently. Old patterns are often firmly entrenched and new patterns are not easy to establish. The True Self cannot be born until the False Self is relinquished. Healthy relationships cannot be born until codependent relationships fall apart. Only the most committed and courageous couples can preside over the death of their unhealthy relationships and then re-create their relationship in a healthy way. However, if the desire is mutual and strong enough, nothing is impossible.

Warning Signs

There is always the possibility that you and your partner may come together to create an equal, mutually empowered relationship and find that you trigger each other in spades. Instead of being the crowning jewel of your life, the relationship becomes the biggest lesson both of you have had.

If this happens, don't feel like a failure. Just get some help. Old patterns of self-betrayal and the wounds behind them sometimes rise up with a vengeance, even after you have done a good deal of healing work.

Below are some of the warning signs you need to be aware of. They indicate that your relationship is off course and may even be unhealthy.

- You frequently blame and shame each other.

- You give away your power/responsibility to the other person.

- You need to control your partner or make decisions for him/her.

- The relationship reinforces patterns of emotional, physical or sexual abuse.

- You can't establish healthy boundaries with your partner.

- You feel responsible for your partner's pain or lack of love.

- You become a victim or a caretaker.

- You often need to be right or to make your partner wrong.

- You are trying to save or redeem your partner.

- You can't bring love to your child or your partner's child.

If one or more of these warning signs are present in your relationship, it may be time to get some help from a trained couples counselor or therapist. It would also be helpful if you would begin to practice the *Affinity Process* with your partner at least two or three times a week. (See my books *Living in the Heart* and *The Keys to the Kingdom*.)

If you are in an unhealthy relationship, it is your responsibility to set clear limits with your partner or get out of the relationship. No one else can take that responsibility for you. But don't hesitate to get help if you need it.

Before making a decision about whether to leave or stay in a relationship, please consider the following suggestions:

- Practice the *Affinity Process* so that each of you can be heard.

- Get therapeutic assistance (marriage/couples counseling) from an experienced therapist.

- When leaving a codependent relationship try to understand and heal the patterns of self-betrayal/victimhood that brought you into the relationship.

- Don't stay in the relationship and suffer.

- Don't leave in anger and blame.

- Treat your partner with respect, kindness and compassion.

- Be responsible for the choices you make.

- Don't try to be responsible for the choices your partner makes.

- Avoid giving or receiving artificial guilt.

- Practice forgiveness of yourself and your partner.

Practicing Forgiveness with Your Partner

Forgiveness is the most important transformational process you and your partner engage in. Practice it on a daily basis. Learn to forgive trespasses and to take responsibility for correcting them. Do this earnestly and consistently or your relationship will shipwreck in the first storm.

When you practice forgiveness, hold yourself and your partner gently. Learn to be flexible and resilient. Admit and apologize for your mistakes. Know that you don't have to be right to be happy. See that you can be wrong and still be loved, and so can your partner.

Unless abuse is present, do not be too quick to leave a relationship that needs work. Take the time to own your mistakes and to begin to model for your partner the change you are asking from him/her.

Realize that no one is perfect. Not you nor your partner. Don't crucify each other. Understand that everyone does the best that s/he can with the consciousness s/he has in the moment. When you learn from your mistakes, you raise your consciousness, and you are less likely to make the same mistake again.

Real forgiveness requires the awareness that you can't change the past. However, you can create a different outcome in the future. So don't waste your time on shame and blame. Ask instead, "How can we make this work better in the future?"

The *Serenity Prayer* helps you to practice forgiveness. It is a great tool that you would do well to use on a daily basis.

Each day and throughout the day take responsibility for what you think, feel, say and do, and ask your partner to do the same. When you are triggered, don't react to the other person. Look inside and see what hidden hurt or belief is coming up for healing. Use your relationship as a mirror to deepen your understanding of yourself. When your partner projects onto you, forgive the trespass. When you project onto your partner, ask for forgiveness.

At least twice this week, when your partner triggers you, ask for an *Affinity Process* space to share what is coming up for you. Follow the *Affinity Guidelines,* and be sure to own your stuff. Make "I" Statements, not "You" Statements. Do not blame your partner or seek to make him or her responsible for how you are feeling. Make it be about you. Let your partner know what wound has been triggered in you and what false belief about yourself you are being asked to look at. Make it clear that no feedback is necessary. Seek only to be witnessed in a loving and compassionate way. Offer to hold the same space for your partner.

Be patient with each other. It takes a while to learn to use this process. The more you do it, the better you will get at adhering to the *Affinity Guidelines* and the safer you will feel communicating honestly with each other.

Eleven Ground Rules for Creating an Ecstatic Relationship

The following ground rules will help you to create and sustain an ecstatic relationship with a life partner.

1. Love yourself unconditionally and learn to be the bringer of love to your own experience moment to moment. Don't depend on others to love you.

2   Establish clear boundaries with others and use the triggers in your relationship as opportunities to continue to heal your core wounds and beliefs.

3. Be ready for intimacy. Before entering a new relationship, take the time to grieve the ending of previous relationships and to heal some of your patterns of self-betrayal.

4. Be sure you really want this relationship. If so, make the relationship your number one priority. Many people say that they do this, but they are just kidding themselves. So ask yourself: "Is work my priority, or children, or caring for my parents?" Be honest. Don't set yourself up for

failure. If your relationship is going to take a back seat to these other commitments, it isn't going to lead to the level of intimacy we are talking about here. Better to set a more realistic goal.

5. Don't be in a hurry. Take your time and be patient. You have to trust the healing process and know that when you have connected sufficiently to your Core Self, you will attract a partner who helps you grow and take the next step on your journey.

6. Surrender the romantic ideal. If you want to attract your soul mate, you need to be realistic and know that s/he will bring up every little unworthiness and self-doubt you have so that you can heal and step into your power and purpose. Seeking your soul mate is unwise if you are looking for an easy relationship that does not challenge your ego structure.

7. Develop a shared vision. Be sure you have similar goals for the relationship and agree on the process you will use to reach them.

8. Consider your partner's needs and experiences as equal to and as important as your own. Many people think they do this, but few really do. This is one of the challenging disciplines of committed relationship.

9. Be monogamous. While it is not impossible to create a full-chakra embrace with more than one person, it is extremely unlikely and unwise to try. On the other hand,

each person must be true to him or herself. In the event that you try to be intimate with more than one partner, honesty and full disclosure are necessary.

10. Avoid blaming or shaming your partner. All attempts to shame or blame are fear driven and will destroy the trust that you have for each other. A successful relationship can be built only through your love and acceptance of each other.

11. Give the relationship the time and attention it needs. An ecstatic relationship requires heart-to-heart communication every day. It requires having fun and celebrating, and it requires honesty and soul searching.

Important Questions to Ask Yourself

A great relationship is a work of art. It is made, not born. You work on creating it moment to moment every day of your lives. To create an ecstatic relationship, ask yourself the following four key questions:

> ➤ Do I really want it? Am I willing to make the relationship the number one priority in my life?

> ➤ Am I ready? Have I sufficiently healed the traumas of my childhood and previous relationships? Am I ready to let the past go?

> ➤ Am I willing? Am I willing to show up for the relationship moment to moment and give it the time and attention that it needs to flourish?

> Am I able? Have I learned to own my fears and hold them with compassion instead of projecting them onto my partner? Am I able to communicate honestly and keep my heart and mind open?

Take some time to consider and meditate on the *Eleven Ground Rules for Creating an Ecstatic Relationship* and the *Four Key Questions* above. Write in your journal about the type of relationship are you trying to create with your present partner or future partner. Consider what degree of willingness, skillfulness, and readiness you are bringing to the relationship. What healing do you still need to accomplish in order for the relationship to transform or for you to be able to attract the relationship you want?

11

~

Follow Your Heart

GOAL

*Find your direction within
and live in the flow of the universe.*

Real Happiness Roadmap

PHASE THREE

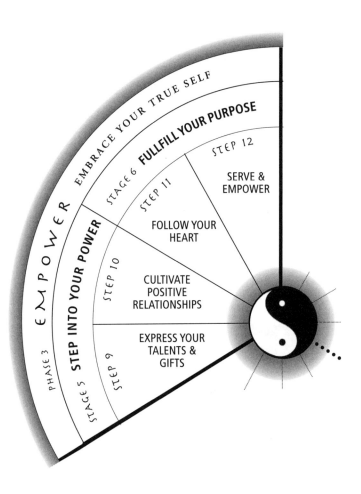

STRATEGY

Be joyful. Stay in the present moment.

Moving From Your Head to Your Heart

In the past, you may have lived primarily in your head, trying to figure everything out intellectually. While this no doubt served you in finding information and problem solving, it did not necessarily help you learn to love yourself or improve your relationship with others. To do that, something else was needed.

You needed to learn to come into your heart, feel your feelings and accept all of your experience. You needed to learn to hold a compassionate space for yourself. You needed to build the inner temple, where you could sit in silence and connect with your intuition and inner guidance. You needed to make friends with your little child and learn to love and accept him or her. You needed to learn to look at your judgments with compassion and to see — without beating yourself up — all the ways in which you gave up your power and betrayed yourself. You needed to take your power back and find forgiveness for yourself and others.

This preparation was essential to bring you into Phase Three of this work. Now, resting in your heart, you are learning to leave the drama of the world behind and listen to the still small voice within. As you learn to trust what you hear and act on it, you gradually move beyond your ego structure and the fears that hold it in place.

A Different Way of Life

All this healing work leads to a different way of life that unfolds from the inside out. It has its own resonance and harmony. Peace within your consciousness translates into peace in your relationships. Love for yourself translates without great effort into love for others. The integration of your shadow translates into compassion for the wounded children of this world who are motivated by fear and driven by insecurity and lack of self worth.

Jesus told us that we need new skins for new wine. So we need to dump out the old wine and recycle the old container. New wine needs a new container. Love and acceptance create a new consciousness. That consciousness is the new container. It holds our experience gently in its embrace.

The new container is created out of an integration of head and heart, reason and intellect, male and female, light and dark, humility and transcendence. It synthesizes the opposites and takes the strengths from both sides.

An integrated life is very different from a polarized life. A polarized life is reactive and volatile. Projection and attack are rampant. The drama is extreme. But an integrated life is quiet and serene. All the judgments are called out and placed on the table where they are held in love and compassion. There is little drama here.

In an integrated life, you are both the witness and the participant. You look within and observe yourself without. You know that everything you see is just information about yourself. Sometimes it seems to be about others, but that is just appearance. Everything you think, feel, say and do belongs to you. Others just hold up a mirror so that you can see the parts of yourself that you haven't been willing to look at.

Inner peace becomes a reality for you as you learn to look at and accept all of your experience. You see that no part of you is bad or evil. There are just parts of you that have not yet been loved. And now you have the skills necessary to bring love to all parts of yourself.

Because you have no enemy within, you don't meet an enemy in the world. All the people you meet are equal brothers and sisters. They have the same fears, the same joys, the same pain and the same joy that you have. Even if they have a different color skin or a different religion, they are human beings just like you. Knowing that, you are not threatened by differences. You learn to love and accept people as they are.

Living in the Flow of the Universe

In the past, your decisions may have been dominated by fear. But now that you know how to hold your fear compassionately, things are different. You are more patient with yourself and others. You no longer speak or act in a hasty or impulsive way. You learn to tune in to what is necessary in each situation, speaking and acting when it feels right to do so, and refraining from speaking or acting when it does not feel right.

Your life begins to simplify. As you take the pressure off, you feel less anxiety, less need to fix or control. Things begin to happen without great effort. As soon as you became aware of a legitimate need, you see that it is met elegantly by the universe. Gradually you realize that when you trust, the flow of abundance moves into your life and helps you move toward your next step, even if you don't know what it is.

You used to need to know everything in advance so that you could plan your life. Now you know that all that is unnecessary. By the time things happen, your plan will no longer be relevant. So you learn to show up with an open heart and an open mind. You trust that when you need to know something, you will be told. You see this happen again and again. In its own strange way, it is completely reliable.

As you let go of your need to figure everything out, grace unfolds in your life. If you need a plan, you make a flexible one, with lots of options. Your job is not to impose your will on life, but to cooperate with life so that your needs and those of others can be fulfilled.

Even when you set a goal you don't know how you will reach it. You don't know whether you will walk, or drive, or take a plane. You don't know when you will arrive or what adventures you will have a long the way. But you trust and begin to move forward however you can. You put one foot in front of another, and somehow things get done. Goals are achieved, even surpassed. And you still don't know how you did it!

Not knowing becomes a real pathway into the divine. You surrender the mind's need to know "how" or "why" or "when" or "where" and just show up when and where you can. You do the best you can and trust that it will be enough. Your best is always enough because you are enough. Everything is unfolding beautifully without you needing to put pressure on yourself or on others.

This is the Great Way of the Tao. It is the Great River flowing downstream. You do not need to push it. You just need to jump in, or get out of the way. It is absurd to think that your job would be to "teach the river" how to flow. Better to be patient and humble and let the river teach you.

There is no better teacher than life itself. And you can be a wonderful student if you will just show up with an open heart and mind. You don't have to decide in advance what will happen or what it will mean. That is just some game the ego plays because it is afraid that its needs won't be met. But you know there is a better way for your needs to be met.

And so you pray: *Lord, let me be an instrument of your will. Let my will and your will be one and the same. Let me trust and show up knowing that you will be with me, guiding my words and my actions, making straight the path before me.*

There is no perfection in the world, but there is perfection in love and the ways of love are beautiful beyond measure. In love, all things are made whole and complete. In love, the Father and the Son are one, and the True Self goes forth into the world in goodness and glory.

The Life of the True Self in the World

The action of the True Self in the world is joyful, enthusiastic, exuberant. Its desire is to give without thought of return and to express itself freely and fully. The words of your True Self are honest and true, and the actions of your True Self are congruent with who you are at the deepest level.

The True Self does great things in this world without great effort or struggle. That is because it is directly guided by the Spirit within.

Of course this cannot happen as long as you are living a selfish, wound-driven life. Then the universal will and the will of your ego will be at odds. You won't move in the flow of the universe. You will swim against the tide. You will struggle and sacrifice.

However, when you surrender your little will to the great universal will, when you stop wanting only what benefits you in a selfish way and start to desire what benefits all equally, there is a major energetic shift that takes place. Now the universe stands with you and behind you, supporting you and moving you forward. The river carries you downstream.

You begin to participate in the abundance of the universe. You become an empty channel, an instrument of the peace and love, as St. Francis called it. You enter a dialog with the divine in which

- you offer your willingness, and it deepens and becomes trust;

- you offer your hope, and it deepens and becomes faith;

- you offer your acceptance, and it deepens and becomes surrender;

- you offer your gratitude for the gifts you have received, and greater gifts are given to you.

The Spirit within guides you to move through the open doors. The people you need to meet show up in your life. The resources you require appear when you need them.

Because you do only what is in harmony with your heart's desire, you live in a state of joy that is contagious and empowering to all who witness it. By living joyfully in the present moment, you shed the limitations of mind that hold you in chains and recreate your suffering. Now that you are living from your heart, new outcomes are possible.

Twelve Practices That Will Help you Keep Love Alive in Your Life.

1. Trust the process (even when you don't know where it is leading).

2. Live in the present moment (not in the past or future).

3. Let things be. Refrain from doing unless guided to act.

4. Remain in silence. Refrain from speaking unless inspired to speak.

5. Stay out of your head. Be okay with not knowing.

6. Stay in your heart and remember to breathe.

7. Cultivate your intuition. Trust your inner knowing.

8. Remain connected with your Core Self (your peaceful center).

9. Bring love when it is needed (whenever fear rises).

10. Let go of judgments, ego agendas and other thoughts or actions motivated by fear.

11. Refrain from forcing. Allow things to unfold naturally, without pressure.

12. Relax, surrender, and give up the need to control.

Living in Love

To live in love is to bring love to yourself and others. It is that simple. When you bring love, love returns to you, for love begets itself. This is the law of supply and abundance:

- First you bring love to yourself.

- Then you extend your love to others.

- And then you receive love in return.

This cycle repeats itself without end. Once love answers the call for love, only love remains. The cries of the wounded child are soothed and pacified, and peace reigns again in our hearts and minds.

Important Questions to Ask Yourself

> Can I stay in my heart and live in the present moment?

> Can I let go of the past and the future?

> Can I surrender my need to control or to know what will happen?

> Can I trust and allow my life to unfold naturally and spontaneously?

> Can I be in touch with my joy and understand that everything works for the good of all?

> Do I realize there is nothing about me or anyone else that I need to fix?

> Can I be peaceful and patient and get in touch with the abundance that is flowing through my life now and at all times?

Spiritual Mastery Prayer

Many people have found my *Spiritual Mastery Prayer* to be helpful in learning to surrender to the Spirit within. I am happy to share it with you here.

Father/Mother God:

Help me to feel my oneness with you
and my equality with my brothers and sisters.

Help me to recognize my judgments
and to look within for correction.

Help me to give up shame and blame
and to learn from my errors
so that I do not repeat them.

Help me to care for my body, my family,
my community and my planet.

Help me to create what is for my highest good
and for the highest good of others.
Help me to be responsible for my creations.

Help me give up victim consciousness
and realize that I am a powerful person
with many creative choices.

Help me to stand up for myself in a loving way
without attacking others or seeking to influence
the choices they need to make.

Help me offer freedom to others
so that I may receive it in return.

Help me reach out with compassion to those in pain,
in grief, under stress, or in limitation of any kind
and offer them hope and encouragement.

Allow my heart to open to them.
Allow my eyes to see beyond the behavior
that is motivated by fear and unworthiness.

May I offer to others and to myself
the unconditional love and acceptance you offer to me.

Help me to master my skills and talents
so that I may place them in your service
and fulfill my purpose here.

Help me to step into the role you would have me play
in inspiring, empowering and uplifting others.

Help me to trust my gifts and give them
without expectation of return
whenever the opportunity arises.

Help me to give freely and love freely,
surrendering the outcome to you.

Help me surrender the need to control
so that I can live spontaneously
and with your grace.

Help me to understand and heal my wounds
so that I don't push love away
or block its presence in my heart
and in my relationships.

Help me soften and become vulnerable.
Help me learn to ask for help
and trust the help that you offer me.

Allow me to heal the past
so that I can enter the present fully.

Allow me to become a doorway
for the healing of others,
and let me walk courageously through the door
that has been opened for me.

Help me surrender what is false
and establish in what is true
firmly and with conviction.

Help me to walk my talk, listen deeply,
and speak only when I have something helpful to say.

Help me to understand that the Friend
is always with me
and my only purpose is to be a Friend to others.

Help me detach from name and fame
and surrender all forms of external authority
so that I can be guided by the authority within.

Allow me to know at all times and in all places
that the highest good of others
is and will always be my highest good.

Let all that separates me from others fall away
so that I may recognize the One Self in all beings.

Allow me to complete my work on earth
with care and humility
and return to you when my work here is done.

May all veils and barriers that separate us dissolve
so that I may dwell fully and completely
in the heart of your love.

Paul Ferrini

STEP

12

Empower Others to Awaken and Heal

GOAL

Be an instrument of love in a world of fear.

STRATEGY

Cook in the sauce. Surrender your ego.

When you reach a certain place in your healing and transformation, you are called to serve and share the work with others. The call may be a formal one or an informal one. It really does not matter. What matters is that your cup is full, and it is time for you to share what you have learned with others.

Once your thirst has been quenched, let others drink from the well. Indeed, be willing to be the bucket that goes down into the well to fetch the fresh water and carry it upwards. It is an organic and natural process to give back to others as you have received. It keeps the energy moving. It enables the gift to be given over and over again to those who need it.

Anyone can be an instrument of the divine when understanding comes and s/he is ready to serve. Sometimes this takes a long time. I tell most of my students that they are like raw meatballs that need to cook a long time in the sauce before they can be taken out and eaten. Many of them try to jump out of the sauce before they are fully cooked. And then when people eat them, they get indigestion.

You can't serve before you are ready. You need to ripen on the vine and cook in the sauce. The longer you cook, the sweeter and more tasty you become. Jesus told us that we would know a good tree by its fruit. In the same way, we know a good teacher by seeing how she acts toward others. If she is gentle and kind, if she is firm when she needs to be, but respectful of others, if she walks her talk and models what she teaches, then we know she is the real deal.

If not, she needs to be go back into the sauce and cook some more. If she isn't willing to do this, that's okay, then she finds another teacher or teaching.

Caterpillars who are unwilling to stay in the transformational sac will not be born as butterflies. Healers who try to heal others before they have healed their own wounds will become wounded healers. Their reputation will follow them. People will know the tree by its fruit.

When the Student is Ready

You have heard the expression "when the student is ready the teacher appears." The opposite is equally true: "when the teacher is ready, the students appear."

Step Twelve asks you to give back to others the understanding and support that you have received. If you have friends, coworkers or people in your community that would appreciate this work, consider facilitating a study group. Come to our *Phase One, Two, and Three Real Happiness Intensives* so that you can be certified to facilitate this work for others. The different types of teacher certification we offer are described on my website www.paulferrini.com.

Even if you are not inclined to share this work formally with others, informal opportunities will arise. People will notice that you are in a healing process, and they will want to know more about it. Don't be afraid to share with them the results that you have experienced.

The beautiful thing about this *Roadmap to Healing and Transformation* is that it is truly universal. All the people you know will be gong through one or more stages in the healing process you have just learned.

As you share your healing with others, your own learning process deepens and intensifies. Sharing what you know is therefore an inevitable next step on the healing journey.

You can best model this work by sharing with others as an equal brother or sister. Acknowledge your humanness and imperfections. Do not put yourself up on a pedestal or claim any special abilities. Your goal must be to empower others to grow and to heal, never to call attention to yourself.

Teachers share well when their cup is full. Then it is easy to give to others. But no one's cup is always full. When you share a lot and don't stay rooted in your spiritual practice, you can feel drained. Your cup can feel empty, and then the words that you speak will seem to fall on deaf ears. You parrot the words, but you cannot back them up emotionally.

That's when you know it's time to refill the cup. It is time to return to your spiritual practice and go deeper in your healing journey. It is time to have the experiences that will challenge you and give you new understandings to integrate into your life. When you have recharged your battery and filled your cup, then it will be time to share again.

A teacher who does not find time to learn burns out. The healer who does not take time for her own healing becomes a wounded healer.

Aside from burnout, the biggest obstacle to sharing this work is perfectionism. No matter how hard you try you are not going to share perfectly. You will make mistakes and learn from them. So take the pressure off. Be humble. Be patient and be gentle with yourself.

Don't stress out or try to do too much. Stay centered. That way it will be easier for you to walk your talk. You are asked not just to teach, but to model the teaching. You demonstrate your healing by the way that you interact with and treat others.

Don't try to be anyone's guru. Don't speak with others in a dictatorial, arrogant, or preachy manner. That would be acting in direct contradiction to the spiritual law of equality on which this teaching is based.

When you share with others, be authentic. Be real. Don't wear a spiritual mask. You are not doing the work to shine at the expense of others, but to empower and inspire others to grow, heal and shine their own light.

A great teacher is not afraid to show her humanness and vulnerability. She freely acknowledges her mistakes and has the capacity to laugh about them. This creates a relaxed and forgiving atmosphere in the class or group.

One of the ways you create safety is by constantly reminding yourself and others that you are not there to try to save, redeem or fix anyone. You are not signing up to heal anyone, but to create a safe space where healing can happen for yourself and others.

Becoming a teacher intensifies your learning process. You don't stop learning when you teach. You learn at a deeper level and at a much faster pace. The student may manage to hide his dirty laundry. The teacher can't.

Your House of Healing

Like others, you do not heal alone. You heal with your brothers and sisters. Specifically, you heal best in community with others who have been wounded in similar ways. This is called your House of Healing. *Alcoholics Anonymous,* for example, is one House of Healing. *Survivors of Childhood Sexual Abuse* is another. There is a House of Healing for every major type of wound.

It helps you to give back if you identify your House of Healing and connect with others in that spiritual family. Once you begin to share with them, you realize just how tuned in you are. People are amazed at what you have learned. They find hope in your example. They realize that if you could heal, so can they. They feel inspired, encouraged and empowered.

Looking back you see there was a purpose to your pain and suffering and to your long and sometimes difficult journey to healing. It prepared you to help others. It prepared you to accept your purpose in life.

Whereas in the past you were part of a chain of abuse that extended from your ancestors to your children and grand-children, now you are part of a chain of healing that extends from your mentors and sponsors down to the community you serve. It is a holy and privileged role, to facilitate healing for others in the same way that it was facilitated for you.

Now it is time to give without any expectations of return or any strings attached. Give because you have something to give and there are people in your city or town who need what you have to give. You aren't doing this to score brownie points or to improve your public image. You are doing it because there is a need that you can fulfill, because there is a heart that is waiting for your kindness, because there is a brother or a sister who will give up if you don't answer his or her call for help.

As you have received, so now can you give. And as you give, you receive deeper and deeper healing. The circle is now complete. But it is not limited. It extends out from your heart to the hearts of all those who need the gift that you have come here to give.

Seven Spiritual Understandings

Working with the Seven Spiritual Understandings below will help you share with others from the heart. It will help you stay connected to your spiritual practice so that your cup remains full and it is easy for you to share with others. You may want to say them aloud for greater impact.

1. I know that everyone is worthy of love at all times.

2. My purpose is to bring love as needed in every situation.

3. I accept my spiritual equality with all beings.

4. I understand that my judgments are delusional and are never justified. All judgments and trespasses are made in fear.

5. When fear grabs me, I recognize it and hold it compassionately. I see the distorted nature of all fear-driven thoughts, words, or deeds, and I refrain from condemning myself or others.

6. I accept responsibility for everything I think, feel, say, or

do. I refrain from thoughts, feelings, words or actions that are unkind or unfair to me or others.

7. Love brings peace, joy and fulfillment. Lack of love brings pain, sadness and lack of fulfillment. In each moment I can choose to give love, not to withhold it.

Important Questions to Ask Yourself

> In what way does my perfectionism hold me back from stepping into my service work?

> Do I share my journey with others in an authentic and loving way or do I show up wearing a spiritual mask and put myself on a pedestal?

> Am I humble and patient or do I have high expectations and put a lot of pressure on myself and others?

> What is the greatest gift that I have to share with others?

> What is the biggest lesson or healing experience I have had in my life?

> What obstacles have I surmounted, what challenges have I faced that might be inspirational for others to hear?

> Am I ready to help others heal and step into their power, or do I need more time for my own healing?

> What is my House of Healing?

> What gifts do I have to give, and what group of people am I most guided to serve?

> Have I reached out to others in my House of Healing?

> If not, would I consider offering an *Affinity Group* for this population as a first step? (See my books *The Keys to the Kingdom* and *Living in the Heart* for more information about *Affinity Group* options.)

Epilogue: The End is Just the Beginning

Our *Real Happiness Workshop* covers the material in this book in an intensive, experiential fashion. It is offered on three long weekends. People who take it have many breakthroughs and experience a powerful sense of community.

Some come to the workshops expecting to finish the work after the last weekend, but when that time comes it becomes obvious to them that in many respects they are just beginning the work. Self healing is a deep and profound work. It does not happen in days or weeks. But the days and the weeks are very important. When you do the three *Real Happiness* intensives, you learn the entire *Roadmap to Healing and Transformation*. You understand where you have been, where you are, and where you need to go. You become aware of the scope of the work and what it is asking from you.

Reading this book also provides you with the *Roadmap* for the journey. But it does not guarantee that you will commit to the journey and take it. In my experience, most people have difficulty staying in their healing process unless they have the support of a transformational community. This is why we encourage you to come and experience this work in person.

It may be that just by reading this book you will begin to

move into a healing process. If that happens for you, understand that the deeper work is calling you. Be courageous and take the next step. Email or call us to find out about the next Real Happiness intensive or Spiritual Mastery retreat.

Hear the call of your own heart and trust it. Come and experience the process at depth with others. Awaken, heal and empower yourself. If you are inspired, become a teacher and share the work with others. The work moves forward only through those who do it. It is entirely experiential. Our teachers not only understand the concepts, they live them and model them. They walk their talk.

I look forward to seeing you at one of my retreats or workshops.

Namaste,

Paul Ferrini

Paul Ferrini is the author of over 40 books on love, healing and forgiveness. His unique blend of spirituality and psychology goes beyond self-help and recovery into the heart of healing. His conferences, retreats, and *Affinity Group Process* have helped thousands of people deepen their practice of forgiveness and open their hearts to the divine presence in themselves and others.

For more information on Paul's work, visit the website at *www.paulferrini.com*. The website has many excerpts from Paul Ferrini's books, as well as information on his workshops and retreats. Be sure to request Paul's free email newsletter, as well as a free catalog of his books and audio products. You can also email: **orders@heartwayspress.com** or write to **Heartways Press, 9 Phillips Steet, Greenfield, MA 01301.**

"35 years of heart-centered spiritual work have taught me what is necessary to bring about a real, lasting change in a person's consciousness and experience."

— PAUL FERRINI

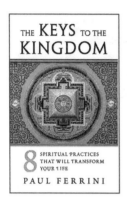

The Keys to the Kingdom
8 Spiritual Practices that will Transform Your Life

BY PAUL FERRINI
ISBN: 978-1-879159-84-6
128 Pages   Paperback $12.95

8 SPIRITUAL PRACTICES THAT WILL TRANSFORM YOUR LIFE

1. *Love Yourself*
2. *Be Yourself*
3. *Be Responsible*
4. *Be Honest*
5. *Walk Your Talk*
6. *Follow Your Heart*
7. *Be at Peace*
8. *Stay Present*

Please use the keys in this book to open the doorways in your life. Take the keys with you wherever you go. Use them as often as you can. They will help you to transform your experience. Fear will drop away and unconditional love will shine through. As you awaken to who you are, so will the people around you.

A fearful world cannot exist for a loving heart. Love changes everything. That is why this works. Do your part, and you will see for yourself.

The Christ Mind books have sold over half a million copies worldwide!

Now Paul Ferrni's Christ Mind Series of books are edited
and unified under one cover. This powerful presentation
of the material is bound to be a bestseller.

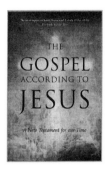

The Gospel According to Jesus
A New Testament for our Time

BY PAUL FERRINI
ISBN: 978-1-879159-82-2
400 Pages   Paperback $25.00

If you know me in your heart, you embody my teaching with
an inner certainty. You know that love is the only answer to
your problems.

When you give love you cannot help but receive it. Indeed,
the more you give, the more you receive. There is no deficiency
of love in the world. Love lives in the heart of every human
being. If it is trusted, it has the power to uplift consciousness
and change the conditions under which you live.

Love is the ultimate reality. It is the beginning and the end,
the alpha and the omega. It emanates from itself, expresses itself
and rests in itself. Whether rising or falling, waxing or waning,
ebbing or flowing, it never loses touch with what it is.

I may not be present here in a body, but I am present in
your love. When you find the love in your heart, you know that
I am with you. It is that simple.

New Book by Paul Ferrini

The long-awaited sequel to *Dancing with the Beloved*

When Love Comes as a Gift
Meeting the Soul Mate in this Life
BY PAUL FERRINI
ISBN: 978-1-879159-81-5
176 Pages Paperback $12.95
ebook $10.00

The soul mate is not just one person, but a work in progress, a tapestry being woven out of light and shadow, hope and fear. Every lover we have prepares us to meet the Beloved. Each one brings a lesson and a gift and each defers to another who brings a deeper gift and a more compelling lesson.

Our partner challenges us to become authentic and emotionally present. S/he invites us to walk through our fears, to tell the truth and to trust more deeply. Gradually, we open our hearts to the potential of creating intimacy on all levels.

And then it is no longer a temporal affair. It is Spirit come to flesh. It is the indwelling Presence of Love, blessing us and lifting us up. It is both a gift and a responsibility, both a promise made and a promise fulfilled.

New Audio by Paul Ferrini

Freedom from Self-Betrayal
Spiritual Mastery Talks at Palm Island

6 CDs $59.95   ISBN 978-1-879159-87-7

Putting Flesh on the Bones
Aligning our Worldly Life with our Spiritual Purpose
Recordings from the 2009 Retreat in
Santa Fe, New Mexico
5 CDs $49.00   ISBN 978-1-879159-80-8

Real Happiness
Awakening To Our True Self
An Introductory Talk by Paul Ferrini
1 CD $16.95   ISBN 978-1-879159-75-4

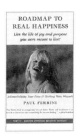

Roadmap to Real Happiness
Living the Life of Joy and Purpose
You Were Meant to Live
Part 1 4 CDs $48.00   ISBN 978-1-879159-72-3

Part 2 3 CDs $36.00
ISBN 978-1-879159-73-0

Creating a Life of Fulfillment
Insights on Work, Relationship and Life Purpose
2 CDs $24.95
ISBN 978-1-879159-76-1

New Audio Releases

Being an Instrument of Love in Times of Planetary Crisis
Two Talks on Individual and Collective Healing
2 CDs $24.95   ISBN 978-1-879159-79-2

The Radiant Light Within
Readings by Paul Ferrini from the *Hidden Jewel* & *Dancing with the Beloved*
1 CD $16.95   ISBN 978-1-879159-74-7

Audio Books

The Economy of Love Readings from *Silence of the Heart, The Ecstatic Moment, Grace Unfolding* and other books.
ISBN 1-879159-56-2 $16.95

Relationship as a Spiritual Path Readings from *Creating a Spiritual Relationship, Dancing with the Beloved, Miracle of Love* and other books. ISBN 1-879159-55-4 $16.95

The Hands of God Readings from *Illuminations, Enlightenment for Everyone, Forbidden Fruit, The Great Way of All Beings* and other books. ISBN 1-879159-57-0 $16.95

Heart and Soul
Poems of Love and Awakening read by the Author.
ISBN 978-1-879159-77-8   1 CD $16.95

Seeds of Transformation:
Set includes: *Healing Without Fixing, The Wound and the Gift, Opening to the Divine Love Energy, The Laws of Love, The Path to Mastery.*
5 CDs   ISBN 1-879159-63-5 $48.00

Two Talks on Spiritual Mastery by Paul Ferrini
We are the Bringers of Love   CD 1
Surrendering to What Is   CD 2
2 CDs   ISBN 1-879159-65-1 $24.00

Love is That Certainty
ISBN 1-879159-52-X $16.95

Atonement:
The Awakening of Planet Earth and its Inhabitants
ISBN 1-879159-53-8 $16.95

From Darkness to Light:
The Soul's Journey of Redemption
ISBN 1-879159-54-6 $16.95

Real Happiness
A Roadmap for Healing Our Pain and
Awakening the Joy That Is Our Birthright
160 pages $12.95
ISBN # 978-1-879159-68-6

Embracing Our True Self
A New Paradigm Approach to Healing Our
Wounds, Finding Our Gifts, and Fulfilling Our
Spiritual Purpose
192 pages $13.95
ISBN # 978-1-879159-69-3

**Real Happiness—
The Workbook**
Creating Your Personal Roadmap
to a Joyful and Empowered Life
96 pages $14.95
ISBN # 978-1-879159-71-6

The Hidden Jewel
Discovering the Radiant Light Within
$9.00
ISBN # 978-1-879159-70-9

Part One: The Laws of Love
A Guide to Living in Harmony
with Universal Spiritual Truth
144 pages $12.95
ISBN # 1-879159-60-0

Part Two: The Power of Love
10 Spiritual Practices that Can Transform Your Life
168 pages $12.95
ISBN # 1-879159-61-9

Part Three: The Presence of Love
God's Answer to Humanity's Call for Help
160 pages $12.95
ISBN # 1-879159-62-7

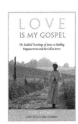

Part Four: Love is My Gospel
The Radical Teachings of Jesus on Healing,
Empowerment and the Call to Serve
128 pages $12.95
ISBN # 1-879159-67-8

Paul's In-depth Presentation of the Laws of Love on 9 CDs

The Laws of Love
Part One (5 CDs) ISBN # 1-879159-58-9 $49.00
Part Two (4 CDs) ISBN # 1-879159-59-7 $39.00

Relationship Books

Dancing with the Beloved:
Opening our Hearts to the Lessons of Love
160 pages paperback $12.95
ISBN 1-879159-47-3

Living in the Heart:
The Affinity Process and the Path of Unconditional
Love and Acceptance
128 pages paperback
ISBN 1-879159-36-8 $10.95

Creating a Spiritual Relationship
128 pages paperback
ISBN 1-879159-39-2 $10.95

The Twelve Steps of Forgiveness
120 pages paperback
ISBN 1-879159-10-4 $10.95

The Ecstatic Moment:
A Practical Manual for Opening Your Heart
and Staying in It
128 pages paperback
ISBN 1-879159-18-X $10.95

Christ Mind Books and Audio

Part 1

Part 2

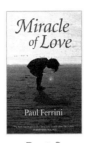
Part 3

Part 4

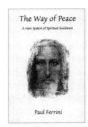

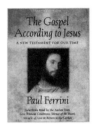

Christ Mind Books

Love Without Conditions ISBN 1-879159-15-5 $12.95
The Silence of the Heart ISBN 1-879159-16-3 $14.95
Miracle of Love ISBN 1-879159-23-6 $12.95
Return to the Garden ISBN 1-879159-35-x $12.95
The Living Christ ISBN 1-879159-49-X paperback $14.95
I am the Door hardcover ISBN 1-879159-41-4 $21.95
The Way of Peace hardcover ISBN 1-879159-42-2 $19.95

Christ Mind Audio Read by the Author

Love Without Conditions 3 CDs ISBN 978-1-879159-64-8 $36.00

The Gospel According to Jesus
Selected Readings from the Christ Mind Teachings
2CDs ISBN 978-1-879159-78-5 $24.95

Wisdom Books

Everyday Wisdom
A Spiritual Book of Days
224 pages paperback $13.95 ISBN 1-879159-51-1

Wisdom Cards:
Spiritual Guidance for Every Day of our Lives
ISBN 1-879159-50-3 $10.95

Illuminations on the Road to Nowhere
160 pages   paperback
ISBN 1-879159-44-9 $12.95

Forbidden Fruit:
Unraveling the Mysteries of Sin, Guilt
and Atonement
ISBN 1-879159-48-1
160 pages paperback $12.95

Enlightenment for Everyone
with an Introduction by Iyanla Vanzant
ISBN 1-879159-45-7
160 pages hardcover $16.00

The Great Way of All Beings:
Renderings of Lao Tzu
ISBN 1-879159-46-5
320 pages hardcover $23.00

Heartways Press Order Form

Name _____

Address_____

City _____State _____Zip_____

Phone/Fax_____ Email* _____

Please include your email to receive Paul's newsletter and weekly wisdom message.

Title ordered	quantity	price

TOTAL _____

Priority Shipping: one book $5.95   _____

Additional books, please add $1.50 per book   _____

TOTAL   _____

For shipping outside the USA, or if you require faster delivery,
please contact us for shipping costs.

Fax Order To: Heartways Press 413-774-9475
Or call 413-774-9474 or 941-776-8001
www.PaulFerrini.com   email: orders@heartwayspress.com

Please allow 1–2 weeks for delivery. Payment must be made by check or
credit card (MC/VISA/AmEx) before books are shipped.

❑VISA ❑MC ❑AMEX _____
              CARD NO.   EXP. DATE